Secrets of Staying in Love

Secrets of Staying in Love

by

RUTH STAFFORD PEALE

Guideposts

CARMEL • NEW YORK 10512

This Guideposts edition is published by special arrangement
with Thomas Nelson Publishers.

Published in Nashville, Tennessee, by Thomas Nelson, Inc. and distributed in Canada by Lawson Falle, Ltd., Cambridge, Ontario.

Printed in the United States of America.

Library of Congress Cataloging in Publication Data

Peale, Ruth Stafford, 1906-
Secrets of staying in love.

Rev. ed. of: The adventure of being a wife. ©1971.

1. Marriage—Religious aspects—Christianity.
2. Peale, Ruth Stafford, 1906- . I. Peale, Ruth Stafford, 1906- . Adventure of being a wife.
II. Title.
BV835.P4 1984 170'.2'0244 84-16506
ISBN 0-8407-5910-X

Dedicated
To My Husband

NORMAN VINCENT PEALE

Who Made It a Joy
To Learn
The Secrets of Staying in Love

With Appreciation to

ARTHUR GORDON

Skilled Writer
for His Valued and
Understanding Assistance
in the Preparation of This Book

Contents

Introduction

ABOUT a year ago, traveling alone, I was flying to California to join my husband, Norman, who had some speaking engagements there. Sitting next to me on the airplane was a young woman, quite pretty and well-dressed, but with a faint shadow of unhappiness on her face. On her slender hands, along with a wedding band, she was wearing some unusual rings—quite exotic ones. When I complimented these, she told me that she worked for a Philadelphia firm of jewelry designers and traveled a good deal demonstrating their specialties. Her name was Jennie, she said with a friendly smile. What was mine?

"Ruth," I told her. "Ruth Peale."

Her eyes widened a bit. "Ruth Peale! Are you Mrs. Norman Vincent Peale?"

I admitted that I was.

"Well!" she said. "This is interesting. I know all about your husband, of course, but I also know a good deal about you." She paused for a moment. "You see, I read your book. The one about marriage."

"That's the only one I ever wrote," I told her, trying to sound modest, but secretly pleased, of course. "I hope you liked it."

"Oh, I did," she said. "It was a very good book. I wanted

to reread it not long ago, but I couldn't find my copy and the bookstore people told me it was no longer available..." Her voice trailed off suddenly and there was something forlorn about the way she turned and looked out the window at the hazy landscape far below.

"Were you looking for something special in the book?" I couldn't help asking.

"Yes," she said in a low voice, "I guess I was."

By now my curiosity was definitely aroused. "Do you feel like telling me what it was?"

"I'm looking for a secret," she said slowly. She glanced directly at me and I saw that her eyes were a clear, candid gray. "Some kind of secret for staying in love."

I thought about that for a minute. No one wants to pry into the private life of a stranger, but something seemed to be telling me that this outwardly poised young career woman needed to talk—wanted to talk.

"You mean," I said finally, "that you're in the process of falling *out* of love?"

Her fingers twisted the narrow gold band on her left hand. "Something like that. Oh..." She made a little deprecating gesture... "It's no big deal, I guess. Happens all the time, as I'm sure you know."

"Yes," I said, "I know, all right. That was one reason I wrote the book in the first place."

"It was a good book," she said again. "One thing that came through clearly was that you and your husband have a wonderful life together. And you said a lot of very useful things about marriage. But I don't recall that you said very much about the problem that so many people have of *staying* in love. Believe me, Mrs. Peale, that's where the real trouble lies. That's at the heart of every broken home in this country—every divorce, every marriage that is really a sham because love has faded."

"Surely," I said, "staying in love is a key element in any good marriage. But there's no single secret, you know. There are many secrets, and it takes a lot of patience, searching, and growing up to discover them and put them to use. I tried to put the principles behind those secrets in my book."

"I know you did," she said. "But I'm a person who needs things spelled out very simply and plainly. One, two, three. Focus on this. Get hold of that. I know the *principles* are important, but I'd just like someone to say, 'Here are ten basic rules for staying in love. Or fifteen. Or twenty. Over here, the do's. Over there, the don'ts.' General discussions are fine, and stories and anecdotes are fine, but I want some rules I can pin up on my mirror and memorize before it's too late. I don't like this feeling that love is draining from my marriage like—like air from a punctured tire! I want to keep the closeness that Jack and I had at the beginning. I'm the kind of person who can't live without love...something in me will just wither and die. And it's beginning to happen, Mrs. Peale. It's beginning to happen!"

There was the shimmer of tears in her eyes, and I found myself feeling very sorry for this young woman. Pure chance, apparently, had dictated our meeting. Or was it pure chance? I believe that God can arrange such encounters when He chooses.

"Jennie," I said, "we've got a couple of hours before we get to Los Angeles. Why don't you tell me a little bit about yourself and Jack. How you met. How you fell in love. Why you think the magic is fading."

So she talked and I listened, while the great tapestry of America unrolled far beneath us. Hers was not an unusual story—I felt it could be duplicated endlessly in towns and cities across the land. She and Jack had met at a marketing seminar. He was four years out of college and she was two. Both were only children in families that had given them many advantages. "I guess," Jennie said pensively, "you could honestly say we were both a little bit spoiled." But they fell in love and married quickly.

They decided to put off having children for a few years because both wanted to establish themselves in careers—Jack was with an advertising agency in Philadelphia and of course she was with the jewelry firm. They seemed to have much in common, and at first everything went very well. But as the years passed and both became more and more deeply involved in their jobs, they began to drift apart. They worked hard and came home tired. They were only social drinkers, Jennie said, but after a drink or two minor frictions had a way of becoming major. Quarrels became more frequent. Jennie's work took her out of town quite often, which left Jack alone. At least she hoped he was alone. "There's a woman in his office," she said, "an account executive about his age who's been divorced. She's attractive and she likes Jack—I can tell. But he gets angry if I complain about the lunches they sometimes have together. He says I'm too possessive. He says I'm imagining things. Maybe I am, but if I really come first in his life, why doesn't he make me feel sure that I'm first?"

On and on she talked, and I found myself liking her and sympathizing with her more and more, caring about her problems that sounded so human and so universal, and wishing I could help her with them. There was something very honest and appealing about her. She didn't try to pin all the blame for their troubles on her husband; she was willing to take some of it herself. Most of all, she valued her marriage and wanted desperately to save it. The trouble was, she didn't seem to know how.

The Rocky Mountains were behind us now and our big silver bird was beginning the long descent that would take us to the edge of the Pacific.

"I've been thinking, Jennie, while you've been talking," I said. "I'd really like to keep in touch with you when we both go back East. I know you're in Philadelphia and I'm in New York, but that wouldn't matter. You could call me on the phone from time to time. Or we could exchange letters. In fact..." I paused because I wasn't sure that I wanted to make the suggestion that had flashed into my mind.

"Yes?" said Jennie expectantly.

"Suppose," I said slowly, "I send you a copy of my book. Suppose we then try an experiment. Every week we'll reread just one of the chapters—each of us reading the same one. At the end of every week I'll write you a letter based on the chapter we've just read, focusing on the secrets you say you're searching for. I'll accent them a bit more, and try to bring some of them close to the one-two-three, do-this, don't-do-that blueprint you were talking about. Maybe that way the basic rules for keeping love alive will stand out more clearly, be easier to learn and to follow. What do you think of that?"

"I think it would be wonderful," Jennie said promptly. "Absolutely marvelous! But wouldn't that be a lot of work and trouble? How many chapters were there?"

"Oh, quite a few," I said, wincing a little at the thought of what I was getting myself into. "But we wouldn't try to cover them all. Besides, my notes to you would be fairly short. They wouldn't attempt to deal with the whole field of marriage the way the book did. They would just zero in on the problem you say you have—the problem of staying in love. We'd be talking to each other like two good friends, one on one. I'm busy, but I'd try to write these little commentaries early in the morning, or late at night, or on trips like this one. It wouldn't be easy, but if I promise to do it, I'll do it."

"But I'd feel so selfish," Jennie objected, "if I were the only one to benefit from an effort like that!"

"Maybe you won't have to be the only one," I said. "Maybe the next time there's a new edition of the book, these extra ideas could be made part of it."

"You mean a new book?"

"I mean a new-old book. The old book has good stuff in it, as you said. This would add another dimension—a kind of plus for the reader."

"Would the new edition have a new title?"

I thought for a moment, "Why not?"

"And what would the new title be?" Jennie's eyes were full of excitement.

I smiled at her. "Why don't you name it?"

She sat up straight. "Something with the word 'secrets' in it. How about..." She hesitated, wrinkling up her nose as she thought furiously. "How about...*Secrets of Staying in Love*? Wouldn't that do it?"

"Yes," I said. "Yes, that would do it."

Dear Jennie,

By now I hope the copy of my book has arrived. I sent it as soon as I got back from California. I thought about you often while I was out there. I told my husband, Norman, all about you. In our family, thinking about a person often includes praying for that person, so you and your problems have been not only on my mind, but also in my prayers. Those prayers are simple ones, Jennie. I pray that God will be with you and Jack – that He will stop the slow disintegration of your marriage, and help you recapture the joy and excitement and tenderness of the early days of your life together.

As you may remember, and as you will see when you start rereading the book, it begins with a challenge flung at me by a young woman in a college classroom right here in the East. I must say, she made a strong impression at the time. I can see her still, slim and self-assured in her designer jeans (she looked as if she had been poured into them), with the clear confident voice of someone who has everything figured out…or at least thinks she has. I've never seen her since that day, but from time to time I wonder what became of her.

Anyway, take a look at what she had to say and what I said in reply. I'll reread that first chapter too, looking for ideas or passages that might apply to some of your problems. Next week I'll write you a note about it.

Meantime, I'll be thinking about you with concern. But also with hope.

Ruth

1

Is Marriage Obsolete?

THE young woman who stood up at the back of the room was a college senior—dark-haired, attractive, sophisticated, a little scornful. "Mrs. Peale," she said, "a moment ago when someone asked you what you considered the greatest career for a woman, you said marriage—right? Well, let's be honest, shall we? It's my opinion—and the opinion, I'd say, of most of my friends—that marriage as an institution is obsolete. We no longer believe that it's possible, or even desirable, to link yourself sexually to one partner in your early twenties and limit yourself to that person for the rest of your life. In fact, we think it's ridiculous."

She paused and looked around at the bright young faces that filled the room. She had their attention, all right. We were in a classroom at a large Eastern university. A friend of mine, a professor of psychology, had invited me to sit in on one of his seminars, ask questions, answer them, and join in the discussion. "It may be a bit rough at times," he had said with a smile, "but I think you'll learn something. And I think my students will learn something from you."

The girl with the dark hair went on coolly: "Take me, for example. There's a boy I'm fond of. We sleep together quite often. I don't think he wants to marry me, and I certainly have no intention of marrying him. He's not my first lover, and I'm sure he won't be the last. But what's wrong with this? Perhaps someday I'll decide I want children, in which case the pressures of society will probably make marriage seem advisable. But until then I want no part of it. And even then I don't intend to be trapped if it goes badly." She shook back her dark hair in a defiant gesture. "We're not blind, Mrs. Peale. We look around and we see what marriage does to people and we don't like what we see. I think when I say these things I'm speaking for a large part of my generation. Do you have any answers?"

All the bright young faces swung in my direction, and I took a deep breath. It was true. I had said that in my opinion marriage was the greatest career a woman could have. I had agreed that a woman might have other stimulating and important jobs, but none was so difficult and demanding, so exciting and potentially rewarding as the job of living with a man, studying him, supporting him, liberating his strengths, compensating for his weaknesses, making his whole mechanism soar and sing the way it was designed to do. I had said this because I believed it *completely*, and I hadn't expected a challenge quite so blunt and harsh as this one. Modern marriage, this independent young woman was saying, was a fraud and a mockery—and she wanted to know if I had an answer.

"Yes," I said to her, "I have an answer, because I'm in the process of living it. I consider myself one of the most fortunate women alive. Why? Because I am totally married to a man in every sense of the word: physically, emotionally, intellectually, spiritually. We're so close that you couldn't put a knife blade between us. I need him and depend on him completely. He completely needs and depends on me. We're not two lonely, competing individuals. We're one integrated, mutually responsive, mutually supportive organism—and this is such a marvelous and joyous thing that nothing else in life can even approach it. It's the greatest of all adventures, but *you'll* never know it. You'll never even come within shouting distance of it if you maintain the attitudes and the code of conduct that you've adopted."

"I don't see why not," she said, but her voice had lost some of its conviction. "Why can't a man-woman relationship be just as meaningful outside of marriage as in it?"

"Because," I told her, "it doesn't have the key ingredients. It doesn't have the commitment. It doesn't have the permanence. It can never achieve the depth that comes from total sharing, from working together toward common goals year after year, from knowing that you're playing the game for keeps. Do you think my husband and I have achieved the relationship we have just by thinking happy thoughts or waving a wand? Don't be absurd! We fought for this relationship! We hammered it out on the anvil of joy and sorrow, of pain and problems—yes, at times, of discouragement and disagreement. But we never thought of marriage as a trap. We thought of it as a privilege. And there's quite a difference!"

The dark-haired girl sat down, and a tall boy in a blue sweater spoke up. "If marriage is all that great, Mrs. Peale," he said, "why is it that one out of four American marriages ends up on the rocks?"

"Any sociologist could give you a dozen fancy reasons," I told him. "I'll give you three quick ones.

"To begin with, a lot of people who get divorced quit too easily. They give up without a fight, because they don't know that what they have is worth fighting for. They give up because they've been allowed to think that everything will be moonlight and roses, when actually it isn't. They give up because unconsciously they've come into the marriage with an escape route already planned, via the divorce court, if everything isn't automatically just dandy. That's one reason why one out of every four marriages winds up on the rocks.

"Another reason is that the women involved aren't using their heads. In this whole area of human relations, women are smarter than men. They ought to be able to study their man, figure out what his needs are—what makes him tick. They ought to help him know where he wants to go. They ought to be able to anticipate trouble and head it off. They ought to be brainy enough and sexy enough to hold a husband. But a lot of them are not, mainly because they're too lazy, or too spoiled, or too busy thinking about themselves and what they're getting or not getting out of their marriages.

"And the third reason is that too many people go around downgrading marriage these days. It has become a favorite indoor sport. The result is that wherever I go, young married women come up to me and bewail their fate. They've been brainwashed into thinking that they're caught in an unrewarding, unstimulating, unchallenging, drab existence. Sometimes I feel like taking them by the shoulders and shaking them, 'Wake up!' I want to tell them, 'Get with it! Here you are, right in the middle of the most fascinating role a woman can play and you don't even know it!'

"You just heard your classmate say that your generation has looked at marriage and doesn't like what it sees. Well, my answer is that your generation hasn't looked very far—or else is seeing only what it wants to see! This country is full of good marriages, built by men and women who know that good marriages don't just happen. They have to be *made* to happen. They know that it takes more brains and determination than some people are willing to invest;

that you have to work at it twenty-four hours a day; that the job is never finished. But when you do, the dividends are enormous. Just enormous!"

Outside in the corridor a bell rang, and I paused, a little out of breath.

"Well," said my professor friend who was conducting the seminar, "that's all for today. Interesting and stimulating, I think. Class dismissed."

The students filed out, some thanking me pleasantly for being with them. One lingered behind—a girl with red hair, not pretty, but with a good-humored, lively face. "Mrs. Peale," she said earnestly, "why don't you make an effort to say to other people what you've been saying to us? I mean, lots of people, not just a handful of students. I think it needs to be said loud and clear. You're obviously so happy in your own marriage, and have made such a success of it, that you ought to tell everyone how you did it and how they can do it."

"I do talk about it," I said, "whenever I get a chance. At church meetings, or at groups like this one, or even now and then on radio or television interviews."

"That's fine," she said, "but the audience is too limited. Besides, people forget what they hear very quickly. Why don't you write a book about your own experiences in marriage? A book that people could read and refer to over and over?"

"I wish I could," I said with a smile. "But in the first place I don't have literary skill or training. And in the second place, I don't know where I'd find the time."

"Think about it anyway," she said. "Just think about it." And she was gone.

Well, I did think about it, all through the rest of the day. I thought about it when the woman I had lunch with told me that her daughter, a fine young woman with two small children, was getting a divorce. Why? Because she and her husband had decided they weren't suited to each other.

"Ruth," my friend said sadly, "I just don't understand it. In the past, when a marriage fell apart, there was usually some well-defined reason: infidelity, or cruelty, or alcoholism, or *something*. But now the virus that causes marriages to collapse seems to be affecting people who used to be considered almost immune: decent people, churchgoing people, intelligent people, and educated people."

I thought about that unhappy woman and her daughter and her two innocent grandchildren as I rode a Manhattan bus down to the corner of Fifth Avenue and 29th Street where the Marble Collegiate Church stands, its slender spire sharp against the sky. My husband, Norman, has been pastor of that church since 1932. I've heard him preach hundreds of sermons from its pulpit. It's a grand old church with a history going back to 1628—actually it's the oldest institution in New York—and I love it, not only for its great tradition, but also for the way it keeps up with the times.

For example, it inaugurated a service known as Help Line, a battery of telephones manned by experts in human relations, most of them volunteers, who answer calls from distressed or troubled people. In its first six months of operation, the Help Line handled thousands of calls, many routine, but some highly dramatic. During my brief visit to the church on this particular day I happened to meet one of the directors of Help Line. "Tell me," I asked him, "what percentage of Help Line calls have to do with marriage problems?"

He thought for a moment. "Too many," he said thoughtfully. "If you include problems like alcoholism or drug addiction that are having a detrimental effect on the caller's marriage, then I'd say the proportion of marriage-problem calls is very high. Why do you ask?"

I told him about my morning at the university and also what my luncheon companion had said. "It left me wondering about the state of modern marriage," I said. "Why is it so shaky? Why are there so many break-ups? Do you have any theory?"

He wrinkled his forehead thoughtfully. "I don't know," he said. "Sometimes it just seems to me that it's a question of pressure. Modern living is so complex. Things happen so fast that sometimes the centrifugal forces in a marriage get the upper hand, and when that happens the marriage begins to break up or fly apart."

The centrifugal forces in marriage...that phrase kept coming back to me as, late in the afternoon, I drove up to Pawling, New York, to join Norman in our old white farmhouse high up on the ridge known as Quaker Hill. A question kept nagging at me: Was there anything that I could do, or say, or write, that might tend to counteract those destructive forces? It seemed presumptuous to think that there might be. And yet...

I didn't mention the matter to Norman until I had finished the supper dishes (the only "help" at the Hill Farm, most of the time, is myself!). We were sitting on the porch, watching the April twilight sift down through the stately maples and the shadows gather in the folds of the Catskills across the valley. Then I told him about my day, about the seminar, about the challenge the dark-haired girl had made. "I know it sounds silly," I said. "I've never tried to write a book. But it was odd how the subject of marriage kept cropping up, wherever I went, whatever I did, all day long."

"Maybe it's not so silly," Norman said. "Maybe you're supposed to do something about all this."

We were both silent for a while. "You know," Norman said finally, "I think an upbeat, optimistic book about marriage might help a lot of people and do a lot of good. You don't have to be very perceptive nowadays to know that we're living in a deeply disturbed world and a terribly troubled nation. Things have changed radically in the last twenty years—and not for the better. One reason, almost certainly, is the state of the modern home, which is a reflection of the relationship called marriage. That's where attitudes and values are formed. If the home is solid, you have a solid society. If it's not, you have crime, divorce, riots, alcoholism, drug abuse...all the things that add up to anarchy."

"Are you thinking about some sort of marriage manual?" I asked him. "That would call for a real expert, wouldn't it?"

"I'm not thinking about a manual," he said. "I'm thinking about a book where you just talk informally about yourself, your marriage, and all the things that go into it. The things we do together. The people we see. The problems we try to solve for ourselves or for others. The trips we take. The arguments we sometimes have that you prefer to call discussions. Anything that comes to mind."

"But I'm not a writer," I protested. "What do I know about writing a book?"

"A lot," he said. "You've helped me with all of mine, every step of the way. You edit my sermons, my newspaper column—everything I write. As for your qualifications, you've had years of learning about marriage simply by living it. We've raised three children who—if I do say so myself—have all turned out well. Not a dropout or a drug addict in the bunch. Now they're all happily married. In addition, over the years, we've listened to hundreds of married couples with every conceivable kind of problem and tried to help them sort out the tangles. You've been as much a part of this as I have. We've done it face to face with troubled people. We've done it in talks and sermons. We've done it by mail, on the telephone, by radio, on television, in books and magazines, on trains and planes and ocean liners. I know you have a lot of valuable techniques and insights, because I've heard you use them."

"I suppose so," I said doubtfully.

"Look," my husband said, "you believe that marriage is a great challenge, a great opportunity, a great adventure. You want to get that message across. So how do you do it? You just tell how that adventure happened to you—to us. Let the reader see us as we really are, just struggling human beings with faults and virtues like everyone else. If you're honest, the reader will stick right with you and learn a lot."

"I don't see how I'd get any continuity into such a book," I said glumly. "It'd just be a collection of bits and pieces, like a...patchwork quilt."

"There's nothing wrong with a patchwork quilt," Norman said cheerfully, "if it's colorful and it keeps you warm."

"But where should I begin?"

"Where did you first start learning the things you want to talk about?"

I had to think about that for a minute. "I guess it was when I had my first job," I said finally, "behind that ribbon counter in the department store in Detroit."

"That's a fine place to start," Norman said. "Who could have a better springboard than a ribbon counter in a department store in Detroit?"

"Well," I said doubtfully, "maybe next week I'll try to start making a few notes."

"If you put this thing off," my husband said, "you'll never start. So you'd better set a specific time. Like tomorrow morning. At seven A.M."

"Seven A.M.!" I cried. "That's when I'm supposed to be making the coffee!"

"Seven A.M.," he said firmly. "I'll make the coffee."

"But suppose I find I can't do it?"

"You used to say you couldn't make a speech, remember? I told you that you could—and I was right. You said you couldn't preside over a public meeting. I told you that you could—and you did. Remember the phrase we've quoted to so many people. *Do the thing you fear, and the death of fear is certain.*"

"It may be the death of *me*," I said sadly.

"We'll risk it," said my heartless husband. "Go and set the alarm clock!"

Dear Jennie,

It's early in the morning here at our farm in the foothills of the Berkshires. The best time of the day, I always think. The winter mornings so stark and still after a fresh snow has fallen, and the summer dawns beautiful with the dew sparkling on the meadows. We love this place – Norman and I – and spend as much time as possible here. Unfortunately, it isn't much.

I reread the first chapter as I promised, with you and Jack in mind. And, you know, the passage that seemed to leap out at me was the one where I'm talking about playing the game of marriage for keeps, where I use the word commitment. That's a strong word, Jennie. One that our ancestors understood a lot better than some of us do. One definition that my dictionary gives is: "an agreement or pledge to do something in the future." In marriage, surely that "something" is to maintain the marriage relationship itself, even when the fires of love have burned low, or are threatening to go out. If you are committed – and that's what marriage vows are all about – you don't give up, you don't quit, you keep going, you keep trying, you keep adjusting because you rule out all other alternatives. Including divorce!

But that's so hard, you may say. Well of course it's hard. At times it's incredibly hard! In that same section, talking about the marriage that Norman and I have, I ask the girl if she thinks we achieved the relationship we have just by waving a wand or thinking happy thoughts? I tell her that we fought for our relationship! We went through all sorts of joy and sorrow, of pain and problems, and even of discouragement and disagreement.

We fought, Jennie, we fought for our marriage. You have to fight for yours too. And if you do, you'll make a great discovery: the more you fight for something, the more you value it. And the more you value it, the more likely you are to win the fight.

So the first secret of staying in love that I'd like to convey to you is simply this: **Be committed**. Be committed to your marriage even when it seems to be going badly. Be committed to the pledge you once made to make it work. Be committed to the idea that God ordained the great institution of marriage and that He wants your marriage not just to "work" but to grow and deepen as the years go by.

If you really make that commitment every day in your mind and heart, the fires of romantic love may flicker and tremble sometimes, but they will never go out.

Be committed, Jennie. Say to yourself every morning when you wake up, "I'm pledged to this marriage. I gave my word. I made a vow before God and I'm not going to break it. I will deal with our problems one day at a time. I will keep on fighting. And in the end, I will win."

I'll write again next week.

With hope and affection,

Ruth

2

Something Of Myself

THE thing I remember most vividly about that first job of mine was the department store customer who gave me such a hard time. She was a sharp-faced woman with bleached hair and a harsh voice, and I can see her now as she pawed through my neatly arranged merchandise at the ribbon counter, complaining, grumbling, criticizing, finding nothing that pleased her—and being quite rude in the process. When I applied for that summer job, I had been told that as far as salespeople were concerned, the customer was always right. It was hard to believe that such an impossible person as this could be right about anything. But I held my tongue. I needed the job, even if it paid only $11 per week. I was only fourteen. I wouldn't be fifteen until September.

When the difficult customer finally moved on after a small purchase, I drew a sigh of relief. As I began sorting my tangled merchandise, I reviewed my performance and even felt a little smug. I had remained calm and polite. I had kept smiling—most of the time, anyway. And after all, I told myself, such people were the exception, not the rule.

I had gotten the job on my own, partly to earn a little spending money, partly to help out at home. My father, a minister, was a man of great kindliness and dignity, but I doubt if he ever earned more than $2,400 a year in his life. My mother, tiny and deeply devout, had a marked musical gift. She played the piano and sometimes gave music lessons that brought in a little extra cash. Both my brothers had paper routes. I remember very well that if one of them was sick, Mother and I would get up at five in the morning and walk the route for him, sometimes in freezing rain or deep snow, folding the papers as we went and tossing them onto porches of houses whose owners—fortunate souls—were still snug in bed. I didn't enjoy being a substitute papercarrier. But delivering the papers was a family responsibility, and in our family that concept was never taken lightly.

My father, who had a strong sense of justice, thought that $11 per week was very little for the store to be paying me, even if I was only fourteen years old. He had advised me to ask for a raise, and (full of qualms) I had done so. The manager had told me that he would think it over and let me know. At closing time that day—the day made memorable by the difficult customer—he called me in and told me that my request was granted. Henceforth I would be paid $13 per week. "And do you know why?" he said. "We sent one of our shoppers to your counter this morning, a lady we use to check on the performance of our salespeople. We told her to be as difficult as possible—and to observe how you reacted. I'm glad to say you passed the test very well indeed."

I don't think my feet touched the ground all the way home. I rushed in and threw my arms around my mother. "I got it! I got it!" I cried, breathless with excitement, and poured out my story. When I told it again at the supper table, my father smiled. "You see," he said, "it pays to be patient and kind, no matter how unfair life may seem to be at the time."

It was a lesson far more valuable than the extra two dollars a week.

I was born in Fonda, Iowa, on my parents' fifth wedding anniversary—Dad always said I was their "wooden-anniversary present." I was the second child in the family, and the only girl. My brother Charles—Chuck, we called him—was three years older. Two years after I was born my brother Bill came along, and the family was complete.

The small towns and parsonages of my early childhood are a blur in my mind. It wasn't until we moved to Detroit when I was seven or eight, and settled in a modest house on Clairmont Avenue, that things began to have a degree of permanence.

As I look back today, my childhood seems like a happy, well-ordered dream. I loved to play jacks on the sidewalks or the porch steps, and I was a fanatical rope-skipper. I walked to and from school, almost a mile, and never considered it a hardship.

There were some wonderful teachers and I still remember them with affection and gratitude. In high school there was Mrs. Watson, our homeroom teacher: white-haired, motherly, a good disciplinarian. I learned something about serenity and self-control just by watching her. Then there was Miss Getamy, demanding but encouraging, who taught public speaking—a rather surprising course to find in a public school in those days.

We had to make three-minute speeches at regular intervals. I can still see Miss Getamy sitting in the back of the classroom appraising each performance, encouraging us in a quiet way. Her practical suggestions, her constant insistence that we learn to think on our feet and not depend on notes, her emphasis on thinking of the class as one person instead of a crowd, all gave me an assurance before people that proved of great help in the years to come.

In my eyes she was always right. One day when I was wearing a green dress she said, "Ruth, you should never, never wear green." And she added, "It makes your eyes turn green." I was crushed. Green eyes! I didn't wear anything green for at least fifteen years. Then one day, looking longingly at a beautiful green dress in a store, I said to the salesgirl, "How lovely," and added wistfully, "but not for me. I can't wear green." "Why not?" the salesgirl asked. "Because," I said repeating Miss Getamy verbatim after a decade and a half, "it makes my eyes turn green."

"What's wrong with green eyes?" the salesgirl asked cheerfully. "Most people think they're distinctive and pretty."

I must have stared at her for half a minute, digesting this momentous news. "They do?" I said incredulously. With some misgiving I bought the dress and never enjoyed anything more! And I have had a green dress in my wardrobe ever since.

But I still wonder, every time I wear green, if Miss Getamy is revolving gently in her grave.

All through my formative years, the sense of family solidarity and security was very strong. We children didn't have many material possessions, but we had the peace of mind and the room to grow that come from a balanced combination of love and discipline inside the home. We had a lot of fun with music. Some of Mother's talent was passed along to all of us, and we spent a lot of time around the piano, harmonizing favorite songs and hymns.

Religion was an important part of our life, but it was not a self-conscious or ultra-pious religion. It was something to be lived, not talked about at length. We said grace at meals. Sunday was a quiet day—no movies, no noisy games. From the start, my own faith seemed as natural as breathing. I never had any intellectual doubts to resolve or great internal conflicts. I simply believed the Christian story and message, and drew strength when I needed it from my prayers and my faith.

Life was simple for children in those days. Home was a place where honesty and decency were taught by example, not by decree. School was a place where good behavior was expected, where patriotism was encouraged, where diligence was rewarded. There were no great class or social distinctions—or if there were, I was unaware of them.

I graduated from Northwestern High School at the age of sixteen and had one year as a freshman at City College in Detroit where tuition was free; all a student had to pay for was books. But then a family dilemma arose. My brother Chuck was at Syracuse University with his senior year coming up. Family finances were strained to the utmost. If Chuck was to get his degree—and everyone agreed that he should—some sacrifices would have to be made. At a family conference a decision was reached: I would drop out of college for a year and go to work to help Chuck complete his education. Then, when he had graduated and landed a job, he would repay me by helping me through three more years of college.

I must say, I was not too happy about this solution. I was only seventeen; I was enjoying myself at City College; I knew that all my friends and classmates would move on without me. But I accepted the plan with as much grace as I could muster, and went to work in the commercial department of the Michigan Bell Telephone Company in Detroit.

I worked there for a little more than a year. The responsibilities of a job made me mature much faster and showed me, in a convincing way, the great advantages of a college education. When I did resume my studies, it was with my proper age group and I went to Syracuse University.

I majored in mathematics. I loved the precision and clarity of figures, the sense that my mind was being trained in systematic thinking and logic. In my junior year, which was my second at Syracuse University, I moved into the Alpha Phi sorority house and had four roommates who shared a study-sitting room. It was there that I first heard about Norman.

I heard about Norman for some time before I actually met him. Girls at the sorority house who went to his church on Sundays came back sighing romantically about the handsome young minister—miraculously unmarried at the age of twenty-nine—who held his congregation spellbound with sermons so eloquent and enthusiastic that going to church became an adventure, not an obligation. They said he emphasized that religion could be a joyous, exciting, life-giving thing. Evidently he had a great sense of humor that appealed particularly to young people. Sometimes waves of laughter swept over the congregation in the great nave of the stately University Church. Outside the church he was said to be friendly, sociable and easygoing. But when he stood up in the pulpit there was also an aura of great spiritual authority about him.

"You really ought to meet him, Ruth," my roommate Phyllis Leonard kept saying. "Or at least come to hear him preach. He's from the Midwest, like you—Ohio, I think. I know you'd like him."

I wonder, sometimes, if the spiritual side of our nature, which is timeless, doesn't have the gift of prescience, of knowing what lies ahead. As Emerson says somewhere, "The soul contains the event that shall befall it." It may be fanciful, but I believe that something in me even then was dimly aware that my destiny was linked with this unseen young man that all the girls were talking about. One night Phyllis asked me to go with her to a party being given by the young people's group at the University Church. Just to stop her from harping on the subject any longer, I went.

It was a gay evening with lots of interesting young people and the time passed very quickly. Phyllis and I were about to leave when she said, "Ruth, you haven't even met Norman Peale. Come on, I will introduce you."

We went across the room and Phyllis said, "Mr. Peale, this is my roommate, Ruth Stafford."

We shook hands. And then a surprising thing happened. He held my hand just a fraction of a second longer than was necessary! I thought to myself, "*This* is going to be interesting!"

And it was. He was a bit embarrassed at calling a young college girl, but he did so quite frequently. He said there were committees on which he wanted me to serve, especially one planning a big banquet for all the college young people, with the famous Ralph Sockman from New York as the speaker. Would I be chairman of the committee?

Planning for this affair, I remember one evening when he asked me to help him arrange the seating at the head table. We worked for quite a while and finally had everyone placed except for two empty seats together. "Who are these for?" I wanted to know. "Well," said Norman, "isn't it amazing? They must be for us!" And so they were.

One day he finally asked me out for dinner—following

the Sunday morning church service. After accepting, I discovered he was to make a commencement speech that afternoon in a town about twenty-five miles away. Did I mind? We could have dinner on the way. I ended up driving the car, so he could concentrate on the last-minute thoughts for his commencement address!

More and more I became aware that he was using me as a sounding board—testing ideas, trying out possible themes for sermons, seeking my reaction. He could be quite self-centered about this at times. I remember one trip to Cazenovia where he was to give a talk that he called "Imprisoned Splendor," all about the shining potentials locked up inside all of us. He told me about it on the way to Cazenovia. He told me again as we had lunch at the old Linklaen House. He gave his talk and it went very well. Then, on the way home, he again suggested I drive. And while I battled the traffic he told me all about "Imprisoned Splendor" for the fourth time!

But I didn't mind. When I saw how stirred his audiences were, how people went away from hearing him uplifted and encouraged, I felt that it would be a privilege to be a part—any part—of the creative process that made such eloquence and effectiveness possible.

As our friendship deepened, though, I began to realize that Norman's eloquence and creativity carried a price tag, and that price tag was a constant vulnerability to self-doubt, a hypersensitivity to any negative consideration where his work was concerned. Once in the early days of our courtship he asked me to tell him frankly what I thought of one of his sermons. So I told him frankly that in my opinion, while the beginning was effective, it sagged off a bit at the end. His reaction was one of complete despair. Overwhelmed with gloom, he told me that I had confirmed what he had long suspected: that he'd never be an effective preacher. He was clearly in the wrong profession. Perhaps he should get out of the ministry before it was too late.

Startled and dismayed, I struggled to correct my blunder...and finally succeeded. But I had learned a lesson that I have had to live with ever since. Namely that the highly creative person does not want objective criticism even when he thinks he does, or when he asks for it. He wants reassurance. He needs help and support in the endless, exhausting battle that he fights with his own merciless perfectionism. Therefore the approach should never be: "That's all wrong," or, "You did that badly." The approach should be: "This is a great paragraph (or sentence, or idea, or approach) that you've got here. Now, what would you think of trying it like this?"

I know that it all sounds a bit laughable, and Norman and I have laughed over it many times. But if, as a somewhat naive college coed, I had failed to learn that lesson quickly and completely and finally, I doubt if we ever would have been married.

Another thing I had to learn (and I truly think God gave me the wisdom, because in those days I had little of my own) was that whatever Norman's basic characteristics were, they were not going to change. He was a grown man, twenty-nine years old, with his character fully formed, all its great gifts and talents and potentials established, but all its defects, too. If I were going to love him (and I was falling as deeply and rapidly in love as a girl ever did), if I were going to share his life and bear his children and help him reach out and transform lives, I was going to have to take him as he was and adapt my own personality to his.

And there was only one way to do this: study the man.

Learn everything about him. Learn to know him better than he knew himself. Learn to analyze his needs as coolly as if they were problems in mathematics that needed solutions. Learn what sort of fuel his personality required for maximum performance, find the right mixture, and supply it.

Our romance progressed swiftly as the days lengthened and the trees showed feathers of green. Too swiftly, I think, for Norman's mother. She came at his invitation to preach the Mother's Day sermon in the University Church. I was impressed. It was clear that much of Norman's gift with words, much of his imagination, much of the romantic element in his makeup came from her.

Unfortunately, Mother Peale was not equally impressed with me. She had great plans, great dreams for Norman. She had accepted the restrictions of life as a small-town minister's wife herself, but she believed her oldest boy had the seeds of greatness in him. She was not unconscious of the value of wealth and social position—and when she looked at me, she could see neither in my family background. She was friendly and polite, but also a bit distant. She didn't directly try to discourage Norman, but she made it clear that if we became engaged she hoped it would be a long engagement. Very long.

It was. After I graduated, Norman helped me find a teaching job. I taught mathematics at Central High School in Syracuse at a salary of $1,800 per year (Norman was making a princely $5,500). All around us the country seemed to be riding a dizzy wave of prosperity as the "Roaring Twenties" drew to a close. But I had to count my pennies carefully.

Two years after I had graduated from Syracuse, Norman and I were married in the University Church in Syracuse on a blue-and-gold June day. I knew as we walked out of the church together that a great adventure was beginning for both of us.

Now, after all these years, I never cease to marvel at what a rich and rewarding pilgrimage it has been.

Dear Jennie,

I'll have to admit to you, a bit sheepishly, that I thoroughly enjoyed rereading that chapter called "Something Of Myself." Ordinarily my life is so full and so busy that I don't have much time for reminiscing. But it was fun to relive those early days of childhood back in Iowa and Detroit, fun to remember school teachers like Miss Getamy and Mrs. Watson, fun to see myself as an eager coed at Syracuse University who was so in love with life – and ultimately with Norman.

I kept thinking, as I read, how lucky I was in those formative years. Not much money, perhaps, and not many material advantages, but such a marvelous balance of love and discipline in the home where my brothers and I grew up. You said that both you and Jack were only children, didn't you? I think perhaps that makes it harder later on to adjust to the inevitable give-and-take of marriage. In the early days, you didn't have to share your toys.

Anyway, the passage I'd like you to ponder is the one where I talked about the importance of being realistic concerning some of your husband's traits – just as he needs to be realistic about yours. I said that I had to learn that whatever Norman's basic characteristics were, they were not going to change. He was already a grown man – twenty-nine years old. His character fully formed. I was going to have to take him as he was.

What about your own marriage, Jennie? Jack is a grown man too, probably about the age that Norman was then. Are you under the illusion that you can somehow force him to change attitudes or habits that you would like to see changed? If so, I think you are facing endless disappointment. There is hope, however.

Change is not impossible. The great thing about human beings is that they can change. But – and this is the key point, I think – they must want to change. The decision has to be theirs. The motivation must come from within. It can't really be imposed from without.

The marriage ceremony recognizes this when it calls upon us to take the other person for better or worse. Acceptance – that's the word, Jennie. Acceptance of the fact that nobody is perfect. We're all fallible human beings with faults and failings that have to be recognized, adjusted to, and compensated for – day after day after day.

Accept your mate. Am I saying that this is the second secret of staying in love? Yes, Jennie, that's exactly what I am saying. Because it is. Accept Jack for what he is.

I'll write again next week.

Ruth

3

Study Your Man

IF I could give one piece of advice to young brides, and only one, it would be this: *study your man*. Study him as if he were some rare, strange, and fascinating animal, which he is. Study him constantly, because he will be constantly changing. Study his likes and dislikes, his strengths and weaknesses, his moods and mannerisms. Just loving a man is fine, but it's not enough. To live with one successfully you have to know him. And to know him you have to study him.

Look around you and decide how many of the best marriages you know are ones where a wife in a deep sense actually knows her husband better than he knows himself. Knows what pleases him. Knows what upsets him. Knows what makes him laugh or makes him angry. Knows when he needs encouragement. Knows when he's too charged up about something and needs to be held back. Knows, in other words, exactly what makes him tick.

On the other hand, the divorce courts are full of women who didn't study their men, who didn't try to anticipate and meet their needs, who failed to observe warning signs while there was still time to do something about them.

Years ago, I remember, we knew a young clergyman whose father was a distinguished bishop. The first time we met him I was mildly surprised to see that, along with his immaculate white shirt and sober dark suit, he was wearing a pair of flaming red socks. This was in the days before men's fashions began to rival the rainbow. The socks intrigued me so that I mentioned them to Norman.

"Yes," said Norman, "they do seem a bit flamboyant, don't they? I understand that some members of his congregation think so too. They aren't happy about those fire-engine socks, and they've told him so, but he wears them anyway."

"Why on earth," I said, "would a quiet, conservative bishop's son do a thing like that?"

"Maybe," said Norman, half joking, "it's to prove that he isn't just a quiet, conservative bishop's son."

The young clergyman was married to a very proper and conventional young woman who was very active in the parish doing all sorts of charities and church work. They seemed, on the surface, quite a well-matched pair. Imagine the sensation, then, when one fine day, out of an apparently blue sky, the young minister left town and took with him the organist of the church, a blonde and lively lady whose husband had died a year or so before. He left a note saying that he was sorry for the scandal he was causing, but that he had stood being a minister as long as he could, that he had found at last a woman who understood him, and that he would marry her as soon as his wife saw fit to give him a divorce. Which she ultimately did.

Who knows how many signs and signals of unhappiness and frustration—aside from his flaming socks—that young man displayed through the years before he made his desperate move? No one can condone what he did, and certainly there are two sides to every story, but in my opinion his wife was probably very, very selfish. She must have had hundreds of indications through the years that her husband was miserable in a profession that no doubt had been thrust upon him by his illustrious father. Under such circumstances, her primary job was not to go around doing good deeds in the community. It was to sense her man's distress and seek a remedy for it. She needed to be more observant.

Studying your man never stops. After our long courtship I felt that I knew Norman inside and out and was ready for anything. But nothing could have been further from the fact.

I soon discovered that in one respect my husband and I were exactly opposite. I never had any problem making up my mind about much of anything, but he had a hard time making decisions: should he accept this speaking engagement, should he go to this meeting, should we accept or decline this invitation, what emphasis should he make in this speech? When he asked for my advice, the questions always seemed to come at the most inconvenient times in my well-planned day. But I would stop and listen patiently. Most of the time he just needed me as a sounding board to help clarify his thinking. And I would go away silently congratulating myself on my patience and understanding, being very glad that the matter was settled.

Many times, to my astonishment, I found the next day that the matter was not settled at all, that he wanted to review it again, that maybe there were angles we had not considered seriously enough. And after another lengthy listening period I would go away realizing his thinking today was almost opposite to his conclusion of yesterday!

Then there were times when plans had been made and I was well along in carrying them out when suddenly Norman would tell me that something had come up to change it all, that this new opportunity was far more important, that we weren't going to do what I thought after all.

This became a major adjustment for me, a fundamental clash in personal characteristics. What could I do? What should I do? Being absolutely honest with myself I knew that Norman's way was often best, that I was too rigid, that if God was going to guide our lives we had to keep our minds open. Norman waited decisions out, and his guidance proved accurate an uncanny number of times.

Well, I have been practicing this for all these years and it is still hard. And I know it always will be. Even today I listened patiently, and I will have to do the same thing tomorrow. Sometimes I think it is such a waste of time. Why can't I change him? Do I have to make this adjustment forever?

The answer is yes. It is never finished.

However, I can say this. If I have developed any real strength of character in my life it is because I realize that only a woman can be a wife, and only a wife can give this kind of help to her husband. No task is as difficult as this, but the rewards are tremendous.

Norman has had to make plenty of adjustments to me—but that is his story.

Some husbands need a wife who entertains beautifully and easily. Some require a gay, lively, fun-loving wife. Some must have a quiet, well-organized home. Norman is one of these. Our home is his only haven in an incredibly busy life. And it must be in perfect order.

Now to me there are some things more important than having everything always in place. It doesn't bother me if the morning newspaper is still on the coffee table at night. But not Norman! His creativity simply stops if anything is out of order.

I studied my husband. He is a public speaker and writer with all the sensitivity—even tension—that seems to go with those talents. He has a practical approach in both writing and speaking, an orderly sequence of ideas. And I gradually came to realize that order in the home or in his office—indeed in his entire conduct of affairs—was essential to his creativity.

So I taught myself to have my entire house in perfect order at all times. (I never knew which room he would look in next!) And I like to think my husband has done a better job in life because I studied these traits of his. Certainly it has brought us close together.

Every bride should be made to realize, somehow, that the way a man feels about a woman depends ultimately on the way she makes him feel. If he has deep needs, emotional, physical, or psychological that he expects her to satisfy, and she fails to satisfy them, it will be very hard in the long run for him to give her the affection, admiration, and loyalty that she needs and wants from him.

Of course, a woman has her needs too, and her husband has an equal responsibility to satisfy them. But I honestly think that in the majority of the cases of marital discord that Norman and I have observed over the years, it's the woman who is failing to recognize and meet some basic needs in the man.

Often it is something as fundamental as sex. We have seen case after case where the husband complains that the wife is too tired, or too busy, to be an adequate sex partner. Almost always, in such cases, the woman misjudges the urgency of the need in her husband. And then she is hurt and astonished when that unfulfilled need impels him to look elsewhere.

Just last week a couple from an upstate town came to ask our help with precisely this problem. They were in their mid-forties, a typical American middle-class couple. Conventional, conservative, soberly dressed, they were the last people you'd expect to find involved in a triangle situation. But they were. The man had been having an affair with a divorcee who lived down the street. The wife, learning about it, had gone to the divorcee's house while her husband was there. There had been a bitter scene with accusations and recriminations. It was clear that the problem was far from resolved. But they wanted us to help them resolve it.

Sometimes these discussions can be brutally frank, and this one was. The woman berated her husband for his lack of loyalty. The husband was not proud of himself, but he was not contrite either. "You," he said, pointing a finger at his wife, "are a dog in the manger. You don't like sex. You never have. But you don't want anyone else to enjoy it!"

"Why don't you act your age?" the wife retorted angrily. "That's all kid stuff, and you know it! People at our stage of life shouldn't have to worry about that kind of nonsense!"

We tried to make the wife see that it wasn't nonsense, that it was precisely this attitude that had driven her husband into the arms of another woman. If she wanted him back she would have to be more understanding and more cooperative. But it was hard going, because in her mind her own preferences came before her husband's needs.

I remember Norman saying to her, "Look, sex in marriage isn't just a physical act of gratification. It's an expression of love, of loyalty, of affection—all the things that I'm sure you yourself want most. Can't you see that?"

"Perhaps," said the woman grudgingly. "But how long can that sort of thing go on?"

"In your case," said Norman cheerfully, "I'd say for at least another thirty years!"

They smiled at that, and you could feel some of the tension go out of the air. They went away, finally, saying that they would try to forget the past and regain the closeness they once had known. And I think they will because the wife admitted her failing and promised to try to understand her husband's needs.

One of the saddest consequences of failing to study your mate, I think, is to have him slowly outgrow you. Not long ago a man came to Norman and said that after twenty-five years of marriage he was going to leave his wife. Norman asked the usual questions: Was there deep disagreement that they couldn't resolve? Was there some other woman in the picture?

No, the man said, it was none of these things. There was no quarrel and he wasn't in love with someone else. But he was bored—bored beyond all reason, beyond endurance. "While the children were still at home," he said, "my wife had something to do—some purpose in life. But now that they're gone, she has none. She has absolutely no outside interests. She has no friends. She talks incessantly—about nothing. She knows nothing about what's going on in the world. I just dread going home in the evening. I can't stand it any longer."

"Can't you share some of your interests with her?" Norman asked. "Can't you draw her into some of your own hobbies or interests?"

"It's too late," the man said. "Maybe if we'd started sharing them fifteen years ago we'd have had a chance today.

But we didn't. We stayed together because we were raising a family, but we were growing at different rates. Now we're two different people, with nothing in common. I'm going to ask her for a divorce." And he did.

The moral is plain enough: studying your mate should include a willingness to participate, at least occasionally, in activities that interest him (or her) more than they interest you. Some domestically oriented women never learn to do this. Their husbands may be ardent golfers, or gardeners, or bowlers, or bridge players, but the women they have married make no effort to join them in the areas where they are happiest and where in most cases they would welcome the companionship of a wife.

Sometimes a pretended interest can become a real one. I knew a woman once, married to a fanatical trout fisherman, who made herself go fishing with him even though she didn't know a dry fly from a luna moth. At first she was horribly bored, baffled by the intricacies of the sport, sure that she could never acquire even the most rudimentary skill. But gradually her attitude changed. Her husband's enthusiasm was contagious; his delight in teaching her was endearing. In the end, although she never became an expert, she was able to participate with an enthusiasm and enjoyment that at first she would have thought impossible. And it all came about because she studied her husband, and tried to make him happy. In doing this, she enlarged her own horizons.

In a way, this also happened to me. When I was first married, I had no real experience or deep interest in church affairs. I knew nothing of board meetings or committee functions. I certainly could not see myself presiding over one. But it soon became apparent that this was an area where I could be of great use to Norman. Studying him made me realize that this sort of activity was not one of his strong points. Organizational work left him impatient and restless. He was at his best when he was preaching, or writing, or dealing with the emotional difficulties of individuals. I began to see that if I could take some of the organizational work off his back, go to the committee meetings, report back, summarize, simplify, help Norman make the big decisions and spare him from having to make the little ones, that I would be making an enormous contribution—one that would make me even more indispensable to him, one that would win his affection and gratitude and esteem for me on an ever-increasing scale.

So I did it. I studied the organizational structure of the church. I learned how to conduct meetings. I practically memorized Robert's Rules of Order. In the process I made a surprising discovery about myself. I was rather good at this sort of thing! People said that I made a good discussion leader, that I had a knack for grasping the essence of a problem, brushing aside irrelevant detail, getting to the point. What began as a slightly apprehensive decision to do something useful for Norman became a whole new dimension in my own life, one that has expanded steadily ever since. When I look back, I am astonished and humbled at the honors in this field that have come my way. My own listing in *Who's Who in America* has nothing to do with being Norman's wife but represents my own career. Thus, when I say that being a wife is the greatest career a woman can have I do it from the vantage point of a career woman.

Having some outside interests of her own will often keep a wife from feeling jealous of her husband's achievements. But she has to keep a wary eye on his masculine ego, which can easily be bruised or damaged. Not long ago I read a magazine article in which a marriage counselor described a situation where a husband became moody and irascible when his wife took a job. "In this case," the marriage counselor explained, "although the husband agreed intellectually with the wife's decision to go to work, he couldn't accept it emotionally. Having a working wife made him feel inadequate as the family provider, so he became defensive and over-sensitive to every real or imagined threat to his masculinity."

I don't mean to imply in any way that it is not perfectly proper for a wife to work. But she will find it very important to study her man's reactions, and not do anything that will lower his self-esteem and in turn damage their marriage.

The wife who studies her husband over the years—really studies him—will come to know him even better than he knows himself. She will be aware of qualities and potentialities in him that he himself may not know are there.

I thought of this the other day when I heard a story about a certain wife in a small midwestern town—a gentle, sweet-tempered woman whose husband was a ladies' man, very attractive to women. He knew it, and he took advantage of it at every opportunity—and there were lots of opportunities.

Since it was a small town, this man's amorous adventures were a matter of common knowledge. And since it was a typical small town, there were those who considered it their duty—their somewhat gleeful duty—to tell the wife about the husband's philanderings.

But the curious thing was that these bearers of ill-tidings never seemed to get anywhere with the wife. She would listen patiently to the worst they had to say, then she would smile and reply that she was quite sure they were mistaken. Her Bob was not that kind of man at all. He would be incapable of such deceit. She appreciated their interest, but they really need not concern themselves further, because obviously they didn't know what they were talking about.

The informers kept trying. But against this serene assurance, against this unshakable faith (for that is what it seemed to be) they made no headway whatever.

Meantime, because nothing remains secret in small towns, reports of his wife's attitude got back to the husband. At first he congratulated himself on having a wife whose suspicions were so hard to arouse. He told himself that it made his extramarital exploits a lot less risky. In fact, it just went to prove his long-time contention that what a wife didn't know wouldn't hurt her.

But gradually a change came over this man. He stopped looking for adventures, and he ceased being responsive when adventurers came looking for him. The townspeople were amazed. One day a man who knew him well asked him what had come over him.

"Well," he said, "I think I could have stood up to any sort of complaint or recrimination from Martha, any wifely jealousy, any amount of anger or accusation. But the one thing I couldn't do was brush off her faith in me. If she thought I was a hero, how could I go on being such a heel? I tried to go on, actually, but I found I just couldn't. I owe her a lot. I'm going to spend the rest of my life trying to make it up to her."

Was that wife simply naive, innocent, and starry-eyed? Or did she know her husband better than he knew himself?

Who can say?

Dear Jennie,

In my opinion the chapter we reread this week – the one called "Study Your Man" – is one of the most important chapters in the book. Nine times out of ten, I think, when marriages begin to go sour, it's because one or both partners have failed really to study the other, really take the trouble to find out what makes their partner tick.

That's a general statement, I know, and you like specifics! Well, in this chapter there is a sentence that's pretty specific. Maybe you should read it aloud to yourself every morning this coming week. It's the one that says, "Every bride should be made to realize somehow that the way a man feels about a woman depends ultimately on the way she makes him feel." Which, I might add, is a truth that cuts both ways – for wives and for husbands.

What have you said to Jack recently that made him feel like a better person, a stronger person, a more worthwhile person, and more of a man? Have any of the following thoughts crossed your mind, and if so have you expressed them in words? Words like:

"I'm proud of you."
"I'm glad to be seen with you."
"My self-confidence is higher when I'm with you."
"I truly believe you put my happiness above your own."
"You make me feel more of a woman."
"You have a wonderful way of making me laugh."
"You keep me from making foolish mistakes."
"I'm so glad you're back."
"I'm grateful to you for so many things."
"I love it when you touch me."
"Thank you for being you."

In every one of those phrases – if only you would utter

them once in a while – you would be saying to Jack "I love you. I love you because you're my mate – my man. I love you because you make me feel happy, warm, secure, wanted, complete, fulfilled, confident, important."

How could he fail to respond with gratitude, with affection, with admiration, with loyalty? He couldn't!

So the third secret of staying in love is this: **Think of your mate before you think of yourself**. For just a little while stop worrying about how Jack makes you feel and ask yourself how you are making him feel. The woman who can do that has learned one of the most important secrets of all in this business of staying in love.

I must go now because there's a minor crisis at my daughter Elizabeth's house. One of the children has a rash and she's afraid it may be measles. I will write again next week. I do hope things are going better for you and Jack. I'll keep praying for you.

Sincerely,

Ruth

4

Fun Is Where You Make It

IT'S astonishing, in this age of wonders, how often people—even young people—come up to me and complain that they're bored. Life is so monotonous, they say. It's dull. It has lost its flavor. Nothing is much fun any more.

Now I know that a share of unhappiness comes to everyone in this life, and it's true that some people have valid cause to be downhearted. But when the average person complains that he's bored, nine times out of ten it's because he isn't making much effort to be anything else. He isn't putting any fun into life, and that's why he isn't getting any out.

It seems to me that all important areas of life should be flavored with fun—marriage, job, housework, friendships, even religion. I've always liked the story of the little boy on his first trip to New York whose parents brought him to a Sunday service at Marble Collegiate Church. The family sat in the gallery where they had a fine view of everything. Norman was in rare form that morning, and his sermon was full of stories taken from everyday life, some of which had their humorous side. The little boy looked down in wonderment at all the happy faces, then turned to his parents. "This can't be a church," he whispered, "everybody's having *fun*!"

Well, why not? Laughter is one of God's most special gifts to man. "Rejoice!" the Bible says over and over. And "A merry heart does good like medicine." One Thanksgiving years ago Norman preached on this topic. The very next Sunday one lively young couple responded to his exhortation to let religion be fun by putting a well-dried turkey wishbone in the collection plate!

One of the chief ingredients of fun is a sense of humor, and most good senses of humor include a sense of the ridiculous. Norman and I still laugh over an episode that happened early in our marriage. Norman was the young minister in charge of the staid and impressive University Church in Syracuse. Somewhat in awe of the dignified deans and erudite professors who were in his congregation, he took pains never to say or do anything unconventional or bizarre. He was always very proper indeed.

One summer afternoon, coming home from the church, he passed by the house of an elderly spinster named Miss Foote, who was also a member of his congregation. Miss Foote was in her front yard looking distractedly for her favorite cat, which apparently had run away.

Norman says that I was forever lecturing him on the importance of always helping his parishioners, no matter what their problem might be. So he offered to help Miss Foote find her cat. "Where did you see it last?" Norman wanted to know. "Right over there," cried Miss Foote. "I think it went through that hole in the hedge!"

The hole was a small one, but Norman gallantly got down on his hands and knees and started crawling through it. Twigs and leaves rained down upon him, brambles pulled his glasses askew, but he kept going until suddenly his head emerged on the far side of the hedge about eighteen inches above a sidewalk. There was no sight of the cat, but on the sidewalk was a pair of feet belonging to a pedestrian who had halted in amazement. Looking up, Norman saw the austere countenance of Professor Perley O. Place, the most imperious and forbidding member of the entire faculty. The gaze of incredulity and disapproval that the professor bestowed upon his spiritual guide and counselor was so paralyzing that Norman couldn't even attempt an explanation. All he could say was, "Good evening, Professor!"

"Extraordinary!" murmured the learned pedagogue frostily. "Most extraordinary!" And he stalked away.

One way to have fun in your life is to associate with "fun" people. Some people carry an indefinable air of gaiety around with them, and they're well worth cultivating, because often that gaiety will rub off on you. We have a friend like that named Millard Bennett. Millard is a jovial soul who often gives lectures at business conventions on the psychology of selling. For a while he and Norman went around giving talks together. Norman always insisted on speaking first, because he claimed that Millard was so good that any speaker who followed him was bound to be an anticlimax.

Millard's favorite topic was persuasion. Anyone, he used to say, could persuade anyone else to walk the road of agreement if only he would use the right approach. "A man," he would tell his audience, "can talk to his wife in two ways. He can say, 'Dear, your face would stop a clock,' and she would be humiliated and hurt. Or he can say, lovingly, 'Darling, when I look at you, time stands still.' " The idea was the same, Millard said, but the way it was phrased made quite a difference!

Millard had one story that went on for at least fifteen minutes about how he persuaded his wife one night, under the most adverse circumstances, to fetch him a glass of water. As he told it, the unsuspecting wife was sorting out some beads on the divan where she was sitting. She had them all classified as to size and color, and the last thing she wanted to do was disturb them, as she would have to do if she stood up. But, ever the psychologist, Millard set himself the problem of persuading her to bring him a glass of water, which he really didn't want at all.

First he told her how pleasant it was to be alone with her on a winter evening with the fire crackling on the hearth. Next he observed that marrying her was probably the smartest move of his life. Then he began to praise her homemaking ability. No one, he assured her, could cook the way she did.

All this time he had been thumbing through a magazine.

"Now, here's an advertisement about a ham," he said. "It looks pretty good, but it couldn't hold a candle to the ones you bake." He sighed plaintively. "By the way, is that ham you cooked yesterday still in the kitchen? A ham sandwich certainly would taste good right now."

Up jumped the proud and happy wife, scattering her beads in all directions, and went into the kitchen to fix the sandwich. Whereupon Millard called out that he had changed his mind. "Don't bother about the sandwich, dear," he said. "But while you're up, would you just bring me a glass of water?"

My telling of the story doesn't do justice to it, but Millard always had his audience in stitches. He was a fun speaker and a fun man.

I've been lucky to be married to a very "fun" man. Norman's sense of the dramatic, his interest in everything, and above all his imagination make him a marvelous companion for people of all ages. When our children were small, for example, Norman spent hours telling them stories that he made up on the spur of the moment, right out of his head. This generally took place at the dinner table and the children could hardly wait. I remember one whole series that went on for months about three imaginary characters named Larry, Harry, and Parry. These remarkable young people had a magic airplane that they kept in their pocket until they needed it. If they wanted to go anyplace they would take the airplane, blow on it and, like magic, it became large enough for them to climb aboard and take off. They would soar away to investigate a big, billowy cloud, or to fight with giants, or to live in the forest in the treetops, or to rescue princesses in distant lands. The magic airplane was a very real and exciting phenomenon to our children.

There was another series of stores about a faintly sinister individual named Jake the Snake, who had an even more malevolent brother known as Hake the Snake. The children would listen, spellbound, to the dreadful deeds of the Snake brothers—and to tell the truth, so would I.

Not everyone, to be sure, has the kind of inventiveness and creativity that can lead so effortlessly to spontaneous fun. But I'm convinced that anyone who will work at it can increase his fun capacity. It doesn't require time or money so much as imagination and the willingness to try something new. Any mother can make a meal more interesting by attempting some exotic or unusual dish. Any father, faced with Sunday afternoon with the children, can think up something interesting or appealing if he'll just put his mind to it. I heard of one busy father who keeps what he calls a "why not?" notebook on his desk at the office. In it he jots down all sorts of offbeat ideas that occur to him during the week. Why not take the children to a farm and try to milk a cow? He says he has only one criterion for such ideas: they have to be fun—or hold the promise of fun.

One winter in New York I took our children on a once-a-week sightseeing or investigating tour—those things you always put off doing. Among other things we went to the New York City bus terminal, the largest in the world with the fastest escalator at that time. We went to the Statue of Liberty and to the Empire State Building. And there were lots of out-of-the-way places. We had a great time.

Sometimes youngsters can get a bit carried away by the spirit of fun. I remember vividly one summer afternoon when our Margaret and John were about ten and eight respectively. I was having a rather serious meeting of churchwomen in our apartment on Fifth Avenue. Suddenly the doorbell buzzed, and there was one of the doormen of the building looking grave. "Mrs. Peale," he said, "there's a policeman downstairs. He has a complaint. Someone is dropping bombs from your apartment windows into the street."

"Bombs?" I echoed incredulously.

"Water bombs," said the doorman. "Paper bags filled with water—and enough sand to make them fall on people's heads."

"People's *heads*?" In the sudden hush behind me I could sense all my churchwomen listening intently.

"Well," said the doorman, "the bombs missed this lady. But it was a near miss. Her clothes are all splashed, and she is very angry. She complained to the policeman. And he is downstairs right now..."

"You mean," I cried, "that our children are dropping these—these things on passersby? How do you know our children are the culprits?" Behind me I could almost *feel* the craning of necks and the raised eyebrows.

"Because, Mrs. Peale," the doorman said resignedly, "your children have been practicing their—er—bombing techniques in the air shaft on the inside of the building. The bottom of the shaft is full of water and sand and paper bags. I'm afraid Margaret and John are the guilty ones. There's no doubt about it."

Well, I had to summon the guilty ones, send them in disgrace to their rooms, go downstairs, placate the policeman, apologize to the irate lady, arrange to pay for having her clothes cleaned, and assure the doorman that such an aerial assault would never happen again.

I had to tell Norman, of course. We spoke to the children sternly, telling them that their prank might have hurt someone or caused a lawsuit. We made them go down to the bottom of the air shaft and clean up the debris. We made them pay out of their allowance for the irate lady's cleaning bill. I forget, now, what other penalties we imposed. But I must confess, one reaction that both Norman and I had, carefully concealed behind our stern parental exteriors, was a feeling of relief and gratitude that our youngsters did have a sense of fun—even if a bit misguided. We were glad that they weren't meek and mild goody-goodies, that they were a pair of high-spirited, fun-loving youngsters, even if they were "preacher's kids."

In too many American homes, I think, parents offer all

kinds of excuses and rationalization for the inertia that is the deadly enemy of fun. They can't be bothered to change the routine, they can't afford to, they can't find the time, it's easier to turn on the television set...and so on.

But all it takes is a tiny spark of originality. For example, one young couple we know, living on a very tight budget, manages to put aside a few dollars a week for what they call their mini-honeymoon fund. When it reaches a certain level, they park their children with friends or relatives, take an inexpensive motel room on the edge of town, dress up a bit, have a carefree dinner, and spend the night together away from all the routine and familiarity of daily living. The wife says that these "mini-honeymoons," which happen three or four times a year, give her such a lift that she wouldn't exchange them for anything.

There are endless ways to break up a pattern of living that has become monotonous. Ask someone you don't know very well to lunch or dinner. Strike up a conversation with a stranger on a bus or a train or a plane (he may learn something, and you certainly will). Try your hand at bowling. Or at wallpapering a room. Fly a kite with a small child. Work as a hospital volunteer. Go and sign up for a course in some subject that has always interested you. Try anything that's new or different.

Of course, breaking out of the prison of routine takes some effort. But there's a wonderful world outside. And sawing through the bars is half the fun and another adventure in being a you-can't-tell-what-will-come-next wife.

Dear Jennie,

Surely I don't have to point out to you the most valuable passage in the chapter we just read. You know as well as I do that it's the story about the couple whose secret for staying in love was the creation of "mini-honeymoons" now and then. Those two people, I think, were very wise. They knew that the pressures of daily living tend to weaken or even destroy the fragile thing known as romance. They also knew that in order to recapture it, very often it's necessary to change the background, alter the environment, create an atmosphere that's different – an atmosphere in which personalities can seem different.

Norman and I once knew a married couple who often traveled together, staying at hotels, when the man was on a business trip. I remember the husband in that case saying that when dinner time came he always asked his wife to go into the dining room first and wait for him for a few minutes. "Then I go in," he said, "and look around, and I see this attractive woman sitting alone at a table. I go over and sit down and look at her as if I'd never seen her before. Now she's not just the person I knew at home – the one with whom I wash the dishes or worry about unpaid bills. She's something more. She's provocative, and mysterious, and desirable. I tell myself that I don't know her completely, that I'll never know all there is to know about her. But she is here, and we have the whole night ahead of us, and I can feel a spark of new excitement beginning to build in me, and I know she feels it too."

That's what they do periodically, this very ordinary but very wise couple. They put themselves into a situation where, for a little while, they can see each other differently. Their secret – and it's a good one – is deliberately to re-create, now and then, an atmosphere in which they can respond to one another with the basic impulses given to them by God Himself.

More precisely, our fourth secret of staying in love

reads something like this: **Create special times for undisturbed romance**.

You might think of trying something like that yourself, Jennie. Suppose, instead of going straight home when you return from one of your trips, you went to a hotel and asked Jack to meet you there. Suppose you made yourself as beautiful as possible. Suppose you waited for him in the dining room, with the key to your room on the table.

Would you recapture something? Perhaps you might.

Good luck, if you do try it.

Ruth

5

Religion—Don't Analyze It—Live It

THE other day I was at a meeting with a group of high church denominational officials. Discussion and wrangling had gone on for hours about certain doctrinal matters. As a matter of fact, the discussion centered around the question of whether or not, in this particular denomination, women should be ordained. Finally one young minister said something that struck a chord with everyone. "Wouldn't it be nice," he said, "if we could just live our religion without arguing about it!"

Well, it certainly would. And it's not only church officials who are guilty of this. There are too many families where religion begins with formal churchgoing, hymn singing, Bible reading, or other strictly ecclesiastical activities...and that's where it ends.

Don't misunderstand me. I know that all these things are important and necessary ingredients in religious faith. But I also think that religion should be simply *lived* as a part of everyday life. It should come to the rescue of people who need help. It should soften all judgments with tolerance and compassion. It should help all members of the family over the hurdles and roadblocks they encounter.

I remember once when Elizabeth came home from school in tears. Some schoolmate whom she considered her friend had been mean to her—or so she said. She was through with Becky, she sobbed. She'd never speak to her or play with her again. She went on and on, pouring out her resentment and anger.

Finally I said to her, "What do you know about Becky's home life?"

She admitted that she knew little or nothing about it.

"Well," I said, "I happen to know that it's not a very happy one. Becky's parents are divorced. Her mother has married again, and Becky doesn't get along with her stepfather. Her real father, whom she loves, never comes to see her. She's an unhappy, confused little girl. Maybe she did act badly toward you, but I don't think it's because she dislikes you. It's because there's great unhappiness and loneliness in her life. So try to be understanding, will you?"

"You mean she's taking it out on me," said Elizabeth, impressed and abashed. "I'll try, Mother, I'll try."

Just a simple little family scene, but I think it shows religion in action in daily life. *Judge not,* says the Bible. That was the lesson, and Elizabeth learned it.

Religion is really love in action. It's caring—really caring—about what another person feels, or says, or is. You don't even have to know the person. Last Christmas a married couple we know took their small children to a store, gave them each some money, and told them to pick out something for a poor child their own age. They were to select it with care because it might be the only present the poor child received. The children were interested at once. Gravely, intently, they went about the business of picking out a gift for an unknown child. Nobody quoted the golden rule to them, but they were following it, and their reward was happiness.

When people truly live their religion, there is every probability that it will rub off on those around them. There was the case of David and Donna Hamilton, two friends of ours who have a Christian marriage in the sense that Christ makes all the major decisions in their life. When there is a dilemma or a problem, they simply turn to Him and ask for help and guidance...and they will tell you with absolute assurance that He never lets them down.

There was the time, for example, when they needed a house close enough to Boston for David to commute to a new job that he had taken. They asked the Lord to help them find a house, and they found one in what seemed to be a pleasant suburb. So they bought it. But as they became acquainted with their neighbors, it began to seem that it was not such a pleasant suburb after all. There was a lot of drinking. There was a lot of extramarital sex. No one ever went to church or had the slightest interest in religion. At neighborhood parties the favorite pastime seemed to be telling dirty jokes.

David and Donna were deeply troubled, but as newcomers they felt hesitant about making their own feelings and attitudes known. Then one night, after attending a party where the storytelling had been particularly loathsome, Donna decided to pray about it. "Lord," she said, "these are all intelligent, well-educated people. Why can't they ever talk about something worthwhile? Why do they have to tell these foul stories? What can we do?"

The answer she got, Donna says, strengthened her conviction that the Lord has a sense of humor. The answer was, "Why don't you try introducing some *clean* funny stories?"

So Donna and David assembled some clean funny stories, and at the next party they told one or two. The results were surprising. "You know," one man said, "it's a relief to laugh at something that isn't dirty for a change. Kind of refreshing, isn't it?"

"That's right," said one of the women. "To tell you the truth, I never did like telling dirty stories so much. But it seemed the thing to do."

So the dirty stories stopped. Then one day a neighbor asked David and Donna where they went every Sunday. "You just seem to vanish," he said.

That gave Donna her opening. "We drive in to Boston," she said, "and go to church. We wouldn't miss it for anything."

"Is that so?" said the neighbor, surprised. "Well, what exactly do you get out of it?"

Quietly, but eloquently and sincerely, David and Donna told him what they got out of it. "I'd like to know more about that," said the man. "And I know a couple of others around here who would too."

As a result, a little group began meeting in the Hamilton home. It grew larger as the word got around that here was something a lot more stimulating than cocktail parties, and a lot longer lasting. The excessive drinking in the community began to diminish. The furtive affairs and liaisons became less common. People began to blow the dust off their morals and their values. Within a year, that community was completely changed—all because two people who really lived their religion shared it with people who had none—and who were hungrier for it than they knew.

Religion—let's stop talking about it, let's stop arguing about it, let's stop analyzing it. Let's just try making it an integral part of the adventure of being a wife.

Dear Jennie,

I wish Norman could write this letter for me. He is the one who lives his religion better than anyone I know. Love is the central element in his life. I've never known anyone who loves life in all its aspects more than he does. He loves people – all sorts of people. He loves places – the rich Ohio farmland where he was born, the gentle Berkshire hills where our farm is, the soaring majesty of the Swiss Alps, the teeming streets of New York or Hong Kong. He loves laughter. He loves his church. He loves the busy life he leads speaking to gatherings of all kinds all over the world. He loves new ideas, new challenges, new problems to solve. He loves his work – preaching, writing, taping radio programs, running Guideposts, raising money for worthy causes, somehow finding time to listen to the problems of people everywhere.

Where does such a torrent of energy and creativity come from? I know what Norman would tell you. He would say that he tries to keep as close as possible to the Source of all energy, and live in such a way that the channels through which that energy comes are always open. He believes that anyone can live that way and receive that energy. That is what he has always preached. Christianity is not just a musty set of ancient beliefs. It's not just a collection of rules. Norman believes that it is a storehouse of endless joy and energy, and the key that unlocks the storehouse is faith.

I don't know how large a part religion plays in your life with Jack, Jennie. We didn't have a chance to talk much about that. But I do know that without it the detrimental forces in marriage are much stronger. Without the conviction that human love is a reflection of God's love, it's much more difficult to stay in love. In other words, the fifth, and probably the key secret of staying in love is: **Keep God at the center of your marriage.**

If you and Jack have drifted away from your faith, that

may have something to do with your drifting away from each other.

I want to end this letter with a prayer that Madame Chiang Kai Shek gave me years ago when we were visiting her at the summer palace in Taiwan. I think you will find it helpful, Jennie if you find a quiet place every morning and read it aloud, slowly. Think about each phrase, believing that you are being listened to and loved by the Creator of all things. Here it is:

A Prayer for a Quiet Time

O Holy Spirit of God,
Come into my heart and fill me;
I open the windows of my soul to let Thee in.
I surrender my whole life to Thee;
Come and possess me, fill me with light and truth,
I offer to Thee the one thing I really possess,
My capacity for being filled by Thee.
Of myself I am an empty vessel.
Fill me so that I may live the life of the Spirit,
The life of Truth and Goodness,
The life of Beauty and Love,
The life of Wisdom and Strength.
And guide me today in all things:
Guide me to the people I should meet or help;
To the circumstances in which I can best serve Thee,
Whether by my actions or my sufferings.
But above all, make Christ to be formed in me,
That I may dethrone self in my heart, and make Him king;
So that He is in me, and I in Him,
Today and forever. Amen.

I'll be praying too.

Ruth

6

Who's The Optimist In Your House?

AT Marble Church on Sunday morning, after the service there is a brunch for members of the congregation. I attend this when I can, and on one occasion I found myself sitting by a woman from out of town. "Oh," she said, "I wish my husband had heard Dr. Peale's sermon. He certainly could use a lift."

"What's the problem?" I asked her. "What's bothering your husband?"

She shook her head resignedly. "Everything bothers him! The state of the world bothers him. The state of his health bothers him. His job and his finances bother him. He's the most downbeat, pessimistic man I know. Life in our house with my husband around is one long gloom."

"Well," I said, "can't you change that?"

"Me?" She looked astonished. "Why, I'm just his wife. What can I do about it?"

"Everything," I said.

"Oh, come now, Mrs. Peale," she said, half disbelieving and half indignant. "It's easy for you to talk. You're married to one of the world's great optimists. You haven't any idea of what I'm up against."

"Oh yes, I have," I answered quickly. "Every wife runs into this problem from time to time and I'm no exception. It's true that my husband is a great optimist. He believes in the goodness of life, and the goodness in people. But he has his moments of discouragement, too. And believe me, his outlook can turn quite dark. When he gets depressed, he sees only the negative side of everything. Sometimes I think he writes about positive thinking because he understands so much about negative thinking! Of course, he does come out of these moods. But I consider it part of my job as a wife to understand all this, to evaluate it unemotionally, and then do something about it."

"Do something about it?" she said with surprise. "What do you do? I mean, how do you help your husband when he is depressed? You almost make it sound as if my husband's pessimism were my fault!"

"Maybe to some extent it is," I said. "I think the wife is the one who can set the emotional climate of the home. Basically, women are more stable emotionally than men—although most men won't admit it. Women are not so vulnerable to disappointment. They're used to soothing hurt feelings and bandaging skinned knees. Ten thousand years ago, when the hunters came back to the cave day after day empty-handed, and the sabre-toothed tiger howled outside, who do you think said, 'Don't worry. Everything will be all right'? Was it the brawny caveman? It was not! It was the cavewoman, and she's been saying it ever since."

"That may be true," my companion said stubbornly. "But I don't think you realize how contagious pessimism can be."

"No more contagious than optimism," I said. "But let's take this problem and go at it logically for a few minutes.

To begin with, is there anything really seriously wrong with your husband's health or his finances?"

"No," she said. "It's all a state of mind."

"All right," I said, "let's consider your tactics. When your husband starts complaining or grumbling or finding fault with things, what's your reaction?"

"Usually I urge him not to be such a complainer. I tell him he's getting me down. I invite him to shut up."

"That's understandable," I said, "but is it wise? Isn't it possible that by shutting him up you're just bottling up all his fear or worries inside of him? Mightn't it be smarter to encourage him to talk, to verbalize all his frustrations, get them out of his system? Maybe one reason he's full of gloom is that he can never truly unburden himself. Maybe you need to learn to absorb some of it for him, as if you were made of emotional blotting paper. That's what I do when my husband gets discouraged. I urge him to talk it out. Believe me, it shortens the period of depression enormously."

"Well," she said, "that makes a lot of sense. But he gets me so upset. I answer him back and before you know it I'm mad and he's mad and it's terrible."

"That isn't being 'emotional blotting paper.' You really have to learn to absorb what is on his mind as he talks it out. Maybe you need some techniques in order to do this."

"Like what?" she asked.

"Oh, there are many. For instance, listen, but don't believe what he says—let it go in one ear and out the other and above all, don't react emotionally to it. Or count to ten. Or look at your husband and think how much you love him. Don't say that aloud. Just think it. And keep thinking of yourself as blotting paper."

"Do you really do it?"

"Yes," I said, "and you can too."

"Is there anything else?" She had fully convinced me that she wanted help.

"Since you ask," I said with a smile, "I'll suggest a few other things. First, stop thinking of yourself as 'only a wife.' You can influence your husband more than any other person in the world. Make up your mind that you're going to help him with this problem, instead of just enduring it.

"Now what, specifically, can a woman with a gloomy husband do? She can try to change his state of mind by changing what goes into his mind. If he were suffering from a vitamin deficiency, you'd change his diet, wouldn't you? Well, you can change his mental diet, too.

"I've noticed that people who are depressed or gloomy seem to enjoy reading or hearing gloomy things. Try to counteract this tendency. If you take the gloom-peddlers at face value nowadays you'd think that the country has failed, society has failed, the church has failed, everything is going to the dogs. But that's just not so. Point out to your husband that it isn't so. Do a lot of upbeat reading yourself so you always have a story to tell that counteracts this kind of news-distortion.

"Next, look for every exciting, hopeful, optimistic item you can find in your daily life and pass it on to your husband. If a preacher says something that gives you a lift, hurry home and tell him what it was. Better still, next Sunday ask him to go with you to hear that preacher! If you come across a story that reflects the innate courage or kindness or determination in people, make sure that your husband knows about it too. Feed upbeat things into your conversation with him. Deep down, he must be hungry for this sort of encouragement. In fact, he must be starved for it!"

"I'm sure he is, poor man," she murmured.

"Most people are," I told her. "Some years ago my husband and I and a friend of ours named Raymond Thornburg started a magazine called *Guideposts*. It has had tremendous success precisely because it fills every issue with true stories of this kind, stories of people who overcome obstacles, who find strength and joy in helping others, who have learned to live positively and happily, who don't let handicaps hold them back or get them down. It's exciting and inspirational and really upbeat all the way. It helps millions of people. It might help your husband too."

"Tell me how I can get it," she said.* "And there's another thing I'm going to do, too. I'm going to try to steer my husband away from people who are downbeat and pessimistic and negative. I'm going to invite positive, clear-thinking people to our home. I can see now that my husband's attitude has attracted a whole lot of pessimists and I'm going to steer him away from them. I can do it and I will!"

"There are a couple of simple exercises," I said, "that you might try—or persuade your husband to try. Just for fun, take a paper and pencil and write down all the good things you can think of about your life together. The human mind can't hold two sets of ideas simultaneously. If you make yourself focus on something good, you can't at the same time dwell on something bad.

"And here's another discipline. For one whole day, try to avoid saying anything critical or derogatory about anybody. You may think something negative about somebody, but don't put it into words. This is harder to do than you might suppose. But if you slip on Monday, try again on

*Write *Guideposts* magazine, Carmel, New York 10512.

Tuesday. Keep trying until you've done it for a whole day. Then do it again. I have a friend who gives up saying derogatory things for Lent. She says that at first she finds it terribly difficult. But after trying conscientiously for forty days, she then finds it almost impossible to say anything negative about anybody."

"Why," said my brunch-companion, "that's a great idea. But for my husband it may be impossible."

"Not if you, yourself, do some of the things we've been talking about," I said. "Not if you really help him."

"It's up to me, now," she said. "I know that. Oh, if I can just get some of this across to my husband!"

"You can," I told her. "There's no reason in the world why you and your husband can't become cheerful, optimistic, outgoing people again. Start thinking that and believing it. Act cheerful and optimistic yourself. Forget about the past with its problems and failures. Live in the present. Make the best possible out of today. Ask God to help and guide you. He will."

The brunch was soon over and it was time to go. "Thanks," she said. "Thanks for everything. I'm going to go home and try to do what you've said."

"Good luck," I said. "I'll pray for you." And I did.

Dear Jennie,

This morning I was looking over the letters I've sent you so far (my wonderful secretary Evelyn Yegella keeps copies of everything). Just for the fun of it I was trying to see if the "secrets" I've been sending you could be condensed into a single word (you said you liked things short and simple).

Well, as you might suppose, some can and some can't.

The first one can be summarized in a single word: **commitment**. If you want love to stay alive there has to be commitment to your marriage vows – unshakeable commitment.

The second was **acceptance**. If love is to last there must be acceptance of the (sometimes harsh) truth that all of us have faults and failings, and that we're not going to change the basic personality of our loved one until he or she wants to change.

The third was really **consideration**. Consideration for your mate's needs, his fears, his anxieties, his desire to be reassured, his yearning for approval, his hunger for self-esteem. Concern for his feelings, a concern so deep that you are willing – most of the time at least – to place his welfare ahead of your own. A concern that will awaken and strengthen his concern for you.

The fourth secret was the maintenance and preservation of **attraction**, the mysterious chemistry that draws men and women together and holds them together through good times and bad. Call it romance. Call it what you will, but it must be protected and defended if love is to endure.

The fifth secret was the power of religious **faith** to undergird human love and give meaning to life itself. I have always liked these lines by the poet Henry Vaughan:

> I saw eternity the other night
> Like a great ring of pure and endless light.

If two people hope to be able to stay in love year after year, and on into eternity, I think that light must shine in their lives together. Steadily. Constantly.

There are the first five secrets I've tried to give you, Jennie: **commitment, acceptance, consideration, attraction,** and **faith**. All rather grand and solemn concepts. Now in this letter I want to talk about a secret that is neither grand nor solemn, but which is important nevertheless. The sixth secret is: **Be a good climate-arranger**.

That, of course, is what I was talking about in the chapter we just read. If you want to stay in love, if you want that love to expand and grow and stay healthy, you have to give it a favorable climate in which to flourish. And in my opinion, the one who determines the emotional climate of the home is – or should be – the wife.

This belief, I must confess, is based on my conviction that in the realm of emotions and human relationships a woman is likely to be more sensitive, more aware, more attuned...in fact, smarter than a man. A woman can manage a man better than the other way around, although I really don't like the word "manage" very much. It sounds too self-centered and domineering, but I think you know what I mean.

With this advantage, though, goes the obligation to keep the climate in the home as favorable as possible. Favorable for everyone. Elsewhere in the book I have told how I work at this. Norman doesn't like clutter – it interferes with his creativity. So I try to keep our home ultra-neat, even though a little disarray now and then doesn't bother me. Also, Norman doesn't like to deal with more than one problem at a time. So I try to arrange his schedule with that in mind. He doesn't like interruptions when he's working on his sermons. So I try to keep Saturdays absolutely clear of all distractions. And so it goes. I feel the climate in which we live is my responsibility, because I'm a better climate-arranger than Norman is.

I wonder if you have ever thought of this, Jennie, and tried to act accordingly. It really is one of the secrets of staying in love, because if the wife understands her role as chief climate-maker, accepts it, and works at it, then that mysterious quality called happiness is more likely to prevail – most of the time anyway.

I hope these little letters are helpful to you, Jennie. Try to remember to be cheerful and optimistic even when you don't really feel like it. You will notice a difference in Jack – I promise.

Your fellow climate-creator,

Ruth

7

This Thing Called Guidance

PEOPLE ask me sometimes if I really believe that there is a supernatural force or power that intervenes in human affairs, sometimes providing answers to problems, sometimes exerting a subtle influence on thought processes, sometimes arranging or rearranging the complex pattern of human existence so that desirable goals can be reached.

I firmly believe that there is such a force and that the correct name for it is God. I believe that He does indeed take part in human affairs. I believe that we can ask Him to do so. And this whole process is something called guidance.

Norman and I both believe implicitly in the availability of divine guidance. We ask for it all the time, in big things and small, sometimes for ourselves, sometimes for others. For years, for example, we asked that all three of our children would be guided to marriage partners with whom they could build strong, happy, successful homes. And those prayers seem to have been answered. We ask constantly for guidance in smaller things too—the little day-to-day problems that come up all the time. At the Foundation for Christian Living in Pawling, New York, Norman and I have adjoining offices. Often Norman will poke his head into my office or call me on the interoffice phone. "Ruth," he'll say, "there's a decision here that has to be made (or a question that has to be answered, or a letter that needs a carefully worded reply). How about coming in here for a minute? I think we should ask for a little help."

When I go into his office, our technique couldn't be simpler. Norman just talks to the Lord as if He were right there (which we know He is) listening. "Lord," he'll say, "we have this problem. You know what it is without our telling You. Please guide us in the right direction. Make us receptive to Your will. We thank You for this help that You are now giving us."

Then we sit quietly for a while. We don't concentrate furiously on the problem or on possible solutions. We try to make our minds quiet and receptive. Sometimes I will think of some appropriate phrase from the Bible, and focus on that. "Be still, and know that I am God" (Ps. 46:10). Or, "In quietness and confidence shall be your strength" (Is. 30:15). After a while one of us will say to the other, "It seems to me that this is the way to deal with this." Or, "I believe we've been on the wrong track with this one. Perhaps we should handle it this way." It's uncanny how often the same conviction will have come to both of us, and how often a clear line of action will open up where things were obscure before.

How can you be sure that you're on the receiving end of guidance? Well, one pretty good indication is when the answer that comes is not the one that you prefer. I think the best example of this in our lives was the time soon after we were married. We were living in Syracuse, New York. Norman was pastor of the University Methodist Church. We were both happy there. We had many friends. Things were going extremely well. Then, suddenly, Norman received calls from two very important churches. One was on the West Coast, in Los Angeles—the largest Methodist congregation in the country. The other came from the Marble Collegiate Church in New York.

Now, as I have hinted before, one of Norman's basic characteristics is indecision—a tendency to vacillate, a reluctance to make up his mind. I think the chief reason is that he has a great gift for seeing all sides of a question. This is a tremendous asset when it comes—say—to counseling a quarreling couple. But it can be a distinct problem in his own personal life when all sides of the question seem to cancel out, leaving Norman on dead center, unable to move in any direction.

This is what happened when the simultaneous calls from two great churches came in. Actually, there were three possibilities—the third being to refuse both calls and stay where we were. But there was no doubt that a greater ministry was awaiting Norman on either the East Coast or the West. The question was which one to accept.

At first Norman did the natural thing, which was to ask the advice and counsel of his family, his friends, and associates in Syracuse. Everyone seemed to have firm opinions and good reasons to back up those opinions. Norman would listen to one set of arguments and lean in that direction. Then a conflicting set would be presented, and he would lean back. He really made up his mind and then unmade it quite a few times. It was a nerve-racking strain not only on him, but on everyone around him. Meanwhile, time was running out. Both churches wanted an answer.

Finally, I remember, one day after lunch I suggested we

go into our living room. After closing the door I said, "Norman, this can't go on. We're not going to leave this room until you've come to a decision. And to come to that decision we're going to do what we should have done in the first place. We're going to put it in God's hands. We're going to ask for His guidance and wait for it and listen for it until we get it, no matter how long it takes."

We stayed in that room all through the afternoon and far into the evening. I remember we knelt at times by an old chintz-covered couch and held hands and prayed. There were long periods of silence. Norman would pace, and I would sit. We both would turn the pages of the Bible. And no answer seemed to come.

All this time I was quite sure what Norman's preference really was. He wanted to go to California. Many things about it appealed to him. He greatly preferred the climate—Norman hates the hot, humid summers of the East Coast. Some of his best-loved college classmates were there. He liked the simplicity and the openness of the people. He was pleased and flattered by the thought of preaching to what was then the largest Methodist congregation in the country, if not the world. He knew he would be happy in California.

As for New York, he seriously doubted his ability to reach or help a sophisticated Fifth Avenue congregation. He was afraid that his popular approach would be frowned upon by people who expected vast erudition or profound theology. He had heard that the great nave of the Marble Church, capable of seating at least twelve hundred people, seldom had a third that many.

Furthermore, he had been told that Fifth Avenue at 29th Street was a bad location—too far downtown. It was said that industry was moving into that area and residents were moving out. That seemed to mean that the church had nowhere to go but down. Finally, the Marble Church was a different denomination—Reformed Church in America. Norman felt that there were no great theological differences, but he had always been a Methodist. His father was a Methodist minister, and there were strong ties of tradition and sentiment to the Methodist Church.

All this was in my mind as we prayed and waited. I knew it was in Norman's mind too. But we tried as hard as we could to surrender any shred of personal preference and leave the whole thing up to the Lord. We must have said, "Thy will be done," a hundred times, if we said it once.

Finally, I remember, the atmosphere in the room seemed to change. Instead of the uncertainty and urgent seeking, a sudden relaxation of tension came. It was almost as if some great silent clock had struck a deep, decisive note. Norman looked at me and said simply, "Do you have an answer?"

"Yes," I said, "I do, but you must make this decision. Have you an answer?"

"I have, indeed," Norman said firmly. "I think God wants us to go to New York." To which I agreed, for the same guidance had come to me.

A few hours before Norman would instantly have cited to me all the good reasons for going to California. But now he seemed sure that New York was where God wanted us.

"In that case," I said, "why don't you pick up the telephone right now and call New York and say you're coming?"

Without a word, he went over to the telephone and put in the long-distance call. Later he told me that all feelings of hesitancy or vacillation were gone. He told the New York official that he would be honored to accept the call to

Marble Collegiate Church. Then he sent a telegram to Los Angeles expressing regret that he could not accept their call. After the days of anguished indecision, there was a calmness and a finality about the whole thing that was simply amazing. No sense of frustration or personal disappointment. Just an acceptance of being led—being guided in the right direction.

Was it the right direction? Well, all I can say is that the powerful West Coast church had to struggle with a downtown location, and finally its great edifice was used for other purposes. In the beginning, things were not easy at the Marble Church either—the dead hand of the Depression lay heavy on the city. But gradually the Power that guided us there saw to it that the empty pews were filled to overflowing, not just once every Sunday morning, but twice. Even worshipers in overflow auditoriums watched over closed-circuit television.

Why did God want Norman to go to New York? I can't pretend to know the mind of God, but it seems at least possible to me that God felt that Norman's message of hope and encouragement and spiritual buoyancy was needed more urgently in New York, where the mood of the people was approaching despair. I think God knew that on weekends in the great impersonal city there were thousands of lonely souls who had nothing to do, nowhere to go, young people who needed a place to make friendships, old people who missed the warm religious ties that they had known in smaller communities. We never gave any thought to such considerations when we tried to solve the dilemma with our fallible human minds. But God knew about them all the time.

In the crowded years that have passed since that night in

Syracuse I have felt this guidance work in our lives countless times. Often it happens right in church on Sunday morning. Time and again, sitting in the pew that I have come to think of as "my" pew, I have heard Norman depart—for no apparent reason—from the outline of his sermon as he had planned to deliver it to make a point that just occurs to him "spontaneously," and then after the service have someone come up to me deeply moved. "Mrs. Peale," they'll say, "that point your husband made in his sermon—you know, he must have been talking just to me, because this problem has been a great burden—and now I know what to do about it."

This happens all the time. What is it? Mental telepathy? I don't think so. I think, consciously or unconsciously, the troubled person comes to church seeking guidance. And I think God uses Norman to provide it.

Very often the person being "used" in these guidance situations isn't aware of it at the time. It's only when you look back that the chain of circumstances leading up to the event suddenly seems more planned and more purposeful than mere happenstance.

I remember, for instance, the time we went to dinner with some friends and afterwards saw a household item in their home that interested us. We asked where they got it and were told where such items were sold in Manhattan. "And by the way," they said, "when you go there, ask for Mr. Benton (a fictitious name). He's the young man who sold us this one. He was very obliging and helpful."

A day or two later during lunch hour Norman and I went around to the store and asked for Mr. Benton. We were told that he was out to lunch. Could anyone else help us?

Ordinarily, we might easily have said yes. But this time,

for some reason, Norman said we'd come back later. As we left the store I said to him, "Why don't we just look now? What difference does it make who sells it to us?"

"Oh," said Norman vaguely, "this Mr. Benton is a friend of the Morgans. There may be some small commission in it for him. It won't hurt us to come back. Anyway, I feel I should see him for some reason."

So late in the afternoon, back we went. Now Mr. Benton had gone down to a warehouse to see about a shipment that had just come in. Could anyone else be of service?

This time I was sure that Norman, not always the most patient of men, would buy the item and be done with it. But again he hesitated. "We'd better come back," he told me finally. "Sometimes these things don't perform the way they should once you get them home. I think it would be better to have someone on this end of the transaction who knows some friends of ours, don't you?"

"You can come back if you like," I said a bit crossly. "I've really got too much to do to keep running in and out of this store looking for Mr. Benton!"

So two days later Norman went back alone. This time he found Mr. Benton in his office. He was a handsome young man, but harassed-looking. "Mr. Benton," Norman said, "my name is Peale. I'm interested in buying your item. You sold one like it to some friends of ours, the Morgans. They send me."

"I know who you are, Dr. Peale," the young man said quietly. "But the Morgans didn't send you."

"They didn't?" said Norman, taken aback.

"No," said Mr. Benton, "God sent you. I'm on the verge of killing myself because I don't deserve to live. I planned to do it last weekend. Then I decided to wait one more week—this week—and ask God one more time to send me help. And here you are."

Norman got up, walked over to the door, closed it. "Tell me about it," he said.

The young man poured out a tragic story about an involvement with his best friend's wife. The friend was in Viet-Nam. The girl had become pregnant. Overwhelmed by guilt and remorse, she had committed suicide. Now her lover felt that he should impose the same punishment on himself. It was one of those poignant and devastating situations that ministers are so often called upon to face.

Calling on all his experience, all his understanding of fallible human beings, all his spiritual insight, Norman was able to bring a measure of peace to the tormented young man and eventually help him start rebuilding his shattered life.

But what brought about that meeting in the first place? What impelled Norman to keep trying until he actually came face to face with the young man? Was it just coincidence? Mr. Benton certainly didn't think so. I don't either. A soul in torment cried out for help, and that help was *guided* to it.

In seeking for guidance, it certainly helps if you are a religious person consciously turning to God. But I believe the power can work even more with nonreligious people, if their objective is a morally valid one and if they will just subdue their own egos and listen.

This whole business of guidance, obviously, is a highly personal thing. No one can prove to anyone else that it exists. All I can do is recommend to anyone who is troubled or uncertain or confused that he ask for it—and see what happens.

It's a free gift. But you have to be willing to accept a gift before you can receive it.

Dear Jennie,

"Anyone who is troubled or uncertain or confused..." That's a phrase from the end of the chapter we read this past week, remember? Is it a description that applies to you? I think it probably does. Certainly you are troubled about your marriage. You're uncertain about the future. And you're confused about what has gone wrong and how it can be set right.

Let's switch back now to the beginning of that chapter. The "supernatural force or power" that I talk about really intervenes in human affairs. Sometimes it provides answers to problems. The "force" is God and He does intervene.

As I've said before, Jennie, I don't know exactly what your religious beliefs may be, but I think that in times of trouble there is a deep-rooted instinct in every one of us that reaches out for help from a power stronger than ourselves.

Jennie, have you ever subdued yourself and really listened to God? Have you ever consciously and consistently asked the force that created the universe for help in your own marital difficulties? Have you hesitated because you think your problems are too small to be of interest to God? I assure you, they are not. He loves you, He cares, and He wants the best for you.

But God does not interfere in human lives, I think, unless He is asked to do so. He stands at the door and knocks, but you must invite Him to come inside. Why don't you do this, Jennie? It's one of the deepest secrets of staying in love.

The seventh secret is very simple. **Pray**.

Your friend,

Ruth

8

When In-Laws Become Outlaws

THE pretty young wife seemed both apprehensive and angry. "Mrs. Peale," she said, "my husband's mother is coming to visit us next week. She's going to stay ten days—ten whole days! And I can't stand it!"

She had approached me in the aisle of the church following the second Sunday morning church service. She identified herself as a member of the church's Young Adult group. Her problem, she said, was one she couldn't discuss dispassionately with her husband. Could she ask me about it?

"Of course," I said, and she told me about the imminent visit of her mother-in-law. "I just can't stand it!" she repeated, and actually stamped her well-shod little foot.

"What is there about it that you can't stand?" was the question I asked her.

"I can't stand the way she tries to manage everything," she said. "From the moment she comes into our house, she just takes over. She has tremendous energy. She's a very positive sort of person. So the way I prepare the meals isn't right; she always knows a better way. My housekeeping isn't well-organized; she keeps telling me to do it differently. No matter how I handle the children, she always has other ideas. By the time she's been in the house twenty-four hours, I feel as if it were no longer mine, but hers. She's my husband's mother, and I know I'm supposed to love her, but, Mrs. Peale, this woman drives me right up the wall."

Then she continued a little more calmly, "She's a widow, and Jack is her only son, so I can't refuse to have her visit us occasionally. But it causes so much friction between Jack and me that sometimes I think we'll get in the habit of fighting. And that is bad. What on earth can I do?"

I knew that Norman had scheduled a meeting with his officers to discuss some church matters, so I had a few minutes to spare. "Let's sit over here in the corner of this pew and talk about it," I said. "There *are* some remedies for this problem of yours. You might find it exciting to try some of them."

It's practically universal, this in-law problem. Very few married couples escape it entirely. Norman and I had our share of it too. We were devoted to each other's parents, but we found them trying at times. Norman felt that my mother was rigid and uncompromising, with little tolerance or understanding of people whose views or standards differed from her own. I had to admit that this was true. On the other hand, I felt that his mother, gifted though she was, could be domineering and possessive. And determined to have her own way.

For example, when we were first married, we always had to go to Mother Peale's home for Christmas. "I may not be here next year," she would say plaintively if I suggested going to my parents or making other plans. So we always wound up going there...and I always had to control and mask my resentment.

Both of us got along better with our fathers-in-law than we did with our mothers-in-law. This also seems to be the general rule; the sharp-edged jokes about in-laws are seldom directed at men. Perhaps this is because fathers are less inclined than mothers to judge or criticize the person their child chooses to marry. Or perhaps their interests are focused on their jobs and not so much on personal relationships. In any case, fathers-in-law seldom seem to generate the kind of friction that mothers-in-law do.

Norman and I were lucky in that from the start we agreed to discuss our feelings about the other's parents openly and honestly—in private. We agreed not to get angry or defensive when the subject of in-laws came up, but to treat it as a kind of good-humored verbal pillow-fight in which either of us could say anything within reason and not do any damage to the fabric of our own marriage.

And it was amazing how often the appraisal voiced was accurate, but never admitted by either of us to ourselves previously. There is always that fine line of fearing disloyalty. But such openness between Norman and me always brought us closer together and made for a depth of understanding that was a great experience every time it happened.

"Your mother is so narrow-minded," Norman would complain. "Why does she have to object to my father's cigars? When she sees him light one, she acts as if she had found him breaking all the Ten Commandments at once. What business is it of hers? Why don't you tell her to cut it out?"

"What she really objects to," I'd reply with some asperity, "is that sometimes when your father's cigars don't taste right, he spits in the fireplace! Why don't you tell him to cut *that* out?"

Or I might say, "Why is your mother so full of fears and phobias about things? She's always sure that the worst is going to happen. She sees a disaster around every corner. I don't want this kind of timidity to rub off on my children the way it did on your brothers and you!"

"My mother's *not* timid!" Norman would counter. "She has a vivid imagination, that's all. At times she thinks you can be pretty callous. She told me that when she was with you in the park the other day, and John fell off his tricycle, you didn't even pick him up. You let some stranger passing by do it!"

"That's right," I'd say. "I knew he wasn't hurt. I wanted him to pick himself up. Your mother acted as if he had broken both arms and legs. That's just what I'm talking about!"

So we'd say to each other anything that came to mind, and I think it was the best possible form of ventilation. I also think that we each secretly wanted the other to defend his parents with fire and sword. After all, a person who doesn't love his parents isn't likely to have much love-capacity in him for a married partner or anyone else.

In talking with a young couple a few days before their marriage, I happened to mention that one of the greatest arts they would have to learn as man and wife was to talk together about each other's parents with absolute honesty and openness. The bride-to-be seemed startled. "Do you really mean that, Mrs. Peale?" she asked.

"Of course I do," I replied. "In fact, I think it's an absolute necessity for harmony and understanding between any husband and wife."

Sally turned to Jim. She held back as though in doubt and then asked, "Jim, do you think we can do that?"

He hesitated, and in a flash I knew that inadvertently I had stumbled onto the thing that could be their greatest problem. He looked at her thoughtfully. It was a long moment, and I could actually feel the hold his mother had on him. Then he said, "Honey, let's do it! Will you help me?"

Over the years, Norman and I have seen more than one marriage founder under the impact of the in-law problem. We have also seen cases where marriages were prevented by pressures exerted by a possessive parent, usually the mother. In one strange case a young woman who had spent her twenties and early thirties looking after a supposedly invalid mother came to Norman after the old lady died. She explained that she had never married because her mother needed her. But now she was haunted by a terrible fear—fear that her mother had been buried alive.

It was one of those cases where the fear is so irrational and so deep that ordinary religious counseling is of little value. Fortunately the psychiatrists at the Institute of Religion and Health were able to help the young woman. One of these doctors told Norman later that the young woman's irrational dread was actually a disguised fear that her mother might not be really dead, and she might still come back from the grave to dominate and warp and twist her daughter's life. It took long and patient therapy to rid the young woman of her morbid obsession.

There was another instance where a young wife came to Norman and told him that she was going to have to divorce her husband. None of the usual reasons for such an attitude seemed to exist. Finally it came out that her mother had disapproved violently of the marriage. "If you marry that man against my wishes," she said ominously to her daughter, "it will be the death of me!" Sure enough, soon after the wedding—which she refused to attend—the old dragon had a heart attack and died. This set up such profound guilt feelings in the daughter's unconscious mind that she came to feel that she could atone for her mother's death only be divorcing her husband. "My mother may be dead," she sobbed, "but her influence isn't. I can still feel her surrounding me, pressuring me. The only way I'll ever be rid of her condemnation is by divorcing my husband. Then maybe she'll leave me alone!"

Sometimes Norman's instincts tell him that the best way to deal with an emotional problem is to be brusque. He said to his tormented visitor, "Listen to me. You are now a married woman. You are supposed to be a mature person. You must stop acting like a frightened child. Your mother is no longer here. She's gone. She's dead. To get rid of these feelings that are troubling you, you don't have to divorce a perfectly good husband. All you have to do is repeat these words after me: 'Mother, you cannot dominate me any longer. You have no control over me. I am living. You are dead. I hereby *command* you to take your cold, dead hand off my life!' "

"Oh, Dr. Peale," the young woman gasped, "I couldn't say a thing like that!"

"Say it!" Norman insisted. "Say it and be free!"

Finally she said it, and such is the power of suggestion that from that moment she *was* free, and was troubled no longer. It was drastic, but it worked.

Sometimes it takes more than the power of suggestion to control a rampaging maternal instinct. A friend of ours once told us of a conversation he had with a distinguished California jurist, Judge Alton B. Pfaff. Judge Pfaff, who for years presided over a Court of Domestic Relations in

Los Angeles, told of a case where a young soldier appealed to him for help. The boy had married a girl who was completely dominated by her mother. She could make no move, no decision without consulting Mom. Everything had to be reported to Mom. Everything had to be approved by Mom.

To a certain type of personality, exercising this sort of power over another person is morbidly satisfying, and Mom had no intention of relinquishing it. At first she insisted that the newlyweds live in her house, where she watched every move with an eagle eye. The son-in-law, naturally, was miserable. Finally he moved himself and his bride into a small apartment, but even there the mother-in-law followed them, appearing uninvited at all hours, sometimes persuading the bride to go back and spend the night with her instead of with her husband.

Finally, to his vast relief, the young soldier was transferred to Arizona. He took his bride with him, and set about starting a new life. But one day he came home to find that his mother-in-law had flown to Arizona, had persuaded her daughter that she was unhappy there, and had actually taken her back to California. It was at this point that the husband, returning to Los Angeles in search of his wife, appealed to Judge Pfaff.

The judge settled the matter by issuing a court order directing the mother-in-law to stop interfering in the marriage and forbidding her to set foot in her son-in-law's house without an invitation issued by him. She was warned that to violate the order would place her in contempt and bring swift and punitive action from the court. So she didn't dare to disobey it. But it took the full power of the judicial system to make her stop wrecking her daughter's life.

In yet another case that we know of, a woman who was a good Christian and a pillar of her church developed a painful limp. No physical cause for it could be discovered; she simply went lame. Her pastor, a wise man, had recently performed the wedding ceremony for this woman's daughter. He knew that she had disapproved of the marriage and deeply resented her new son-in-law.

In a long talk with the woman, the minister told her that he thought her limp might well be the reflection of a twisted condition in her mind. "I'm afraid you're guilty of sin," he said, "the sin of despising another human being. I believe you hate your son-in-law, although he has done nothing to deserve your condemnation. I believe you have this limp because something deep within you knows that you are not walking uprightly in your heart, and so you can't walk uprightly in your everyday life."

The woman's eyes filled with tears. "You may be right," she said. "What can I do?"

"I want you to come to the church with me," the pastor said, "and kneel at the altar. I want you to confess this sin of anger and hatred, and ask for release and forgiveness. I want you to take Communion and resolve to make a fresh start. Then I want you to go to your son-in-law and admit your fault and ask for his forgiveness too. I believe that if you will do the first few things, the last will not be so hard."

Actually, it was very hard, but the woman did it. She went to the nearby town where her daughter and son-in-law lived. She rang the doorbell. When the son-in-law came to the door, she managed a tremulous smile. "I'm your wicked mother-in-law," she said, "come to ask your forgiveness for many things."

He was a perceptive young man. He didn't say a word.

He just gave her a hug and drew her into the house. From that point on, they were friends. And the minister must have been right about the limp, because it disappeared.

Norman has a somewhat similar mother-in-law story that he loves to tell about the man whose mother-in-law lived in the same house. The man came to Norman claiming that she was driving him crazy, not because she was interfering or domineering, but because she was ruining his breakfasts. Every morning, he said, he liked to get up and have a cup of coffee alone in the kitchen. But every morning his mother-in-law would come scuffing downstairs in an old bathrobe with curlers in her hair and heelless slippers on her feet which made a horrible dragging sound when she walked. She never said anything worth listening to. She would pour herself a cup of coffee and drink it with loud slurping sounds. Like a horse, the man said. And not only that, but when she sat at the table she would maddeningly scrunch her toast. One more scrunch, the man said, one more slurp, and he was going to commit murder...or else leave his own home for good.

"Well," Norman said to him, "I can give you a solution to your problem. But I doubt if you're brave enough to attempt it."

"Try me!" said the man. "I'll do anything. I promise!"

"All right," Norman said. "Tomorrow morning, when you're about to leave for work, turn back from the door and say casually to your mother-in-law, 'Mother So-and-so, how about having lunch with me today downtown, just the two of us?' "

The man stared at Norman as if he had lost his mind. "You must be joking," he said.

"Not at all," Norman replied, "and make it the best restaurant in town. Remember, you promised you'd do anything."

With many misgivings, but because he was a man of his word, the son-in-law took Norman's advice. To his amazement, when his mother-in-law appeared at the restaurant, she was a completely different woman, well-groomed, alert, intelligent, good-humored, a highly agreeable luncheon companion. Why? Because like all of us, she responded to attention, to being treated like a woman instead of like an undesirable piece of furniture. A completely new relationship was established, and it went on for many years.

The moral of the story—and this is probably the best single rule for anyone facing an in-law problem—is this: stop thinking of your marriage partner's relatives as a special breed known as in-laws (a term with faintly unpleasant connotations) and think of them simply as human beings with flaws and imperfections but also lovable qualities. Just discard the in-law label in your mind. Think of them as people. Treat them like people!

This was what I told the young wife who accosted me at church that Sunday. But I said some other things, too. "You tell me that your mother-in-law is full of energy and tends to take over. Instead of resenting this, why don't you turn it to your advantage? Which aspects of housekeeping do you dislike? Ironing? Sewing? Why not plan to have a small mountain of ironing on hand and ask your mother-in-law to do it for you? Do you need curtains made, or slipcovers? Get the material and leave it in her room. And while she does the work, get out of the house and do something with your husband. If she insists on taking over, let her take over tasks that you'd rather avoid anyway!"

I said another thing to the girl. "Instead of resenting your mother-in-law, why don't you make a study of her—a calm, thorough, objective analysis of what makes her tick? That's what I did with my mother-in-law. I tried to figure out what made her the way she was. I tried to understand her motives and her actions. In the process I learned an amazing amount about my husband and why *he* was the way he was. After all, Norman's mother had been the strongest influence in his life before I met him. Trying to understand her helped me to understand him.

"Finally," I continued, "you can turn this whole thing into a challenging exercise in controlling your own emotions. You're a member of this church; well, put your faith to work! Learn to forgive your mother-in-law for her intrusive or domineering ways. Remind yourself that she means well. Remember that if you're patient and kind with her, your husband will know it and appreciate it and love you all the more for it. Stop thinking about her visit as ten days of misery. Take it an hour at a time. Stop wringing your hands and stamping your foot and saying 'I can't stand it.' Tell yourself calmly that you can stand it and you will stand it and that you can even profit by it."

She thanked me and said soberly that I had given her some good and much-needed advice, and that she would try to do as I had said.

Before I leave this chapter, which seems to deal mainly with mothers-in-law, I might add a few words on the art of being one. It only takes one wedding ceremony to turn a mother into a mother-in-law, and this has happened three times to me.

The basic rule, as everyone knows, is to *be willing to let go*. To open that tight parental hand and set the child free, free to move surely and happily into a new life in which the parent can no longer be dominant. If it's your daughter who has married, you have to remember that she has a new identity, a new decision-making role. Don't give unsolicited advice, even when it seems to be needed. If you catch yourself doing it, as I admit I often have, bite your tongue and stop—in mid-sentence if necessary.

If your son has married, remind yourself that you no longer have a direct line into his life. A new situation exists, a triangle situation, which is much more complex. Look for something to praise in your daughter-in-law every time you're with her. If your son hears you speak well of the woman he has chosen, it makes him feel proud and happy, and strengthens the ties he still has with you.

When grandchildren start coming along, love them and admire them, but don't make suggestions about how they should be brought up. You may have your doubts, but it's better to keep them to yourself. I'm startled, myself, at the way *my* children seem to neglect *their* children's table manners. They seem to me to be extremely messy eaters. But theirs is a new generation, with new standards and new points of view. Who am I to say that I am right and they are wrong?

I'll make one firm point, though. If grandchildren are left in your house, then they are under your discipline and should conform to your standards. This can be a rude awakening for some youngsters, but there's no reason why an older person should be victimized in her own home by behavior which she does not wish to tolerate.

A friend of mine had her two grandchildren for some days, a little girl of nine and her younger brother, age six. The boy was getting into everything and paying no attention to his grandmother's warnings. Finally she said, "Johnny, if you disobey me once more, I will not take you out for lunch with your sister and me. You will have to stay home."

He understood, but paid no attention. At noon the grandmother took her little granddaughter and left the house amid screams from Johnny.

When she returned he came meekly to her and said, "Grandma, why didn't you give me a spanking like Mommy does and *then* take me out to lunch with you?"

Finally, I believe that a good-humored and fair-minded mother-in-law can be a great help to the people who marry her children by giving those people the benefit of her long experience in dealing with those children. All people have quirks and faults, and who knows them better than their own mother? Thus, I remember, I told Paul Everett, before he married our Margaret, that Maggie could be quite sharp-tongued and sarcastic at times...and he had better be prepared for this.

I told Lydia, who married our John, that she would have to get used to John's tendency to pounce on innocent words or phrases and try to read unintended meanings into them. I told John Allen, who married Elizabeth, that at times she could be hypersensitive and get her feelings hurt too easily, but that these reactions never lasted long. And I really think these little insights helped minimize potential areas of friction or misunderstanding in those marriages.

So...in-laws are not really outlaws; they're just plain, everyday people linked together in a relationship that is a bit more complicated and demanding than it would have been if somebody's daughter hadn't married somebody else's son.

The best formula for getting along inside that relationship? The same one that works in any relationship. It's called the golden rule.

Dear Jennie,

As I read the chapter about in-laws I found myself wondering what I might find that could be helpful to you. After all, getting along with your in-laws and staying in love with your husband seem to be two very different things. And yet, there may be a connection and I believe that connection exists because in studying my own mother-in-law, I learned a great deal about Norman himself.

Did it ever occur to you that most of the lovable things about Jack and at least some of the unlovable things come straight from his parents? After all, they created him in a very literal sense. Genetically, he is a blend of both of them, which means that he has inherited many traits from both. They are also the ones who created the environment in which Jack grew up. You told me yourself that both you and Jack were only children, and you added wryly that probably both of you were a bit spoiled. If that's the case – and it may well be – both sets of parents have to take some of the blame.

Very often, I think, if you study your father-in-law or your mother-in-law and discern certain traits that you don't particularly admire, it's easier to be a bit more tolerant when those traits appear in your husband. A young wife came to me recently complaining that her husband was selfish and inconsiderate. He liked to go directly from work to the golf club where he spent a couple of hours playing cards with his bachelor friends before coming home. "I've had to be at home all day with the baby," she said. "I want Philip to come home to us. The way things are now, he comes home, wolfs his dinner, then either watches television or goes to sleep on the sofa. I hardly see him at all! Is this the way a husband is supposed to act?"

"No," I said, "it sounds to me as if Philip is acting like a married bachelor, not a husband." So we discussed her problems at length, and gradually it emerged that

Philip's mother had accepted it, but Philip's wife did not. In the end we were able to help them work out some compromises that probably saved their marriage. Once the wife realized that, in a sense, her husband had been programmed to act that way, she was a little less angry and a little more understanding.

Study your in-laws, I know that doesn't sound very thrilling, Jennie, but it is the eighth of the secrets of staying in love.

With affection,

Ruth

9

The Indispensable Art Of Wifely Persuasion

"MRS. Peale," the young woman said, "I love my husband, but he's as hardheaded as a mule. He's the stubbornest man alive. When we disagree about something, it always has to be settled his way. When we argue, I never seem to get my point across. And I'm sick of it! Last night we had a knockdown, drag-out fight. Believe me, if we have many more like that, our marriage is going to wind up in the trash can!"

She was a pretty little thing with dark, expressive eyes that flashed as she remembered the events she was telling me about. I was in Boston for a meeting, a friend had kindly arranged a luncheon, and this young wife was seated next to me. She was a friendly, outgoing person. Evidently this problem with her husband was weighing on her mind, because she seemed anxious to tell me all about it. "He's a mule!" she repeated. "An ornery, balky, hammer-headed mule! One more row like that, and I'm going to walk right out of the house. I mean it, Mrs. Peale, I really mean it!"

"Well," I said mildly, "it's possible to have a disagreement without having a fight, you know. What were you disagreeing about?"

"Oh," she said disgustedly, "it was about our summer vacation. Paul is a great outdoorsman; he likes to go up to Nova Scotia and fish and camp out. Well, that's all right. He works hard. He's starting his own advertising agency, and it's a struggle. He needs to get away for a while. But we went to Nova Scotia last summer. And the summer before that. This year I want to go down to my parents' place on Cape Cod. I love it there. It's where I spent the happiest days of my childhood. I know lots of people, and I can't help it if I prefer people to chipmunks and bears. My parents have a cottage on their place that we can have rent-free. It's cool and civilized and wonderful, and it's where I want to go!"

"Does your husband dislike Cape Cod?" I asked her.

"No," she said. "Not really. But he's one of these men who likes to keep on doing whatever he's *been* doing. He loves whatever is familiar. He hates to try anything new. And it's not fair! I thought about it all day yesterday, and the more I thought, the madder I became. So as soon as he got home from work, I let him have it. 'Paul Johnson,' I said to him, 'whether you like it or not, we're going to Cape Cod this summer. Not to Nova Scotia. And that's that!' "

"And how," I asked, "did he react to this—er—greeting?"

"He blew up. He said some awful things, and so did I. This morning was even worse, because he didn't say anything. Not a word. He just got up and drank some instant coffee and went to work." She looked at me and I could tell that this spirited, sophisticated young wife was miserable and frightened. "Oh, Mrs. Peale," she said, "what shall I do? Can you help me?"

"I think so," I said. "You're not the only woman in the world who's married to a stubborn man, you know. You're just going to have to try to master a subtle and tricky art, one that's an absolute *must* for any woman who wants her marriage to succeed. I had to learn it myself, the hard way. You can learn it too."

"What is it?" she demanded eagerly.

"Persuasion," I said. "The indispensable art of wifely persuasion."

I waited a moment for that to sink in. Then I continued: "Have you ever stopped to think how essential this thing called persuasion is, not only in marriage but in life? It's involved in just about everything that matters. You can't force anyone to be your friend. You can't make anyone love you or marry you. You can't compel anyone to hire you, or give you a raise. No matter how much authority you may have, you can't just bark orders and hope to get things done. There has to be a winning of acceptance, of agreement, of cooperation. There has to be successful persuasion—and there are certain rules for accomplishing this."

"Rules?" my luncheon companion repeated. "What rules?"

"The first rule," I said a bit drily, "is *timing*. Last night you broke that rule—smashed it into smithereens. Let's review the situation. Your husband comes home. You said he works hard, so we can assume he's tired. He's looking forward to a happy reunion with the woman he loves, a pleasant dinner, a restful evening. He opens the front door, and bang! As you put it, you let him have it. An ultimatum, on a touchy subject, before he's even had time to take off his hat! Now, an ultimatum is always a mistake, because it leaves everybody out on a limb with no way to climb down. But you weren't thinking about that. You were just thinking about yourself and what you wanted and how unfairly you've been treated. So you hurled your ultimatum. And your timing was terrible."

"Yes," she said slowly, "I guess it was."

"The second rule in the art of persuasion," I continued, "has to do with *self-interest*—the other fellow's. If you have a proposal, you've got to make him see what's in it for him. The other day in a speech my husband quoted something that Edmund Burke, the great English statesman, once said: 'What you make it the interest of men to do, that will they do.' I think that Mr. Burke was putting his finger on one of the great secrets of persuasion.

"But did you make a summer on Cape Cod seem like something that would be to your husband's advantage? You could have, you know. You might have pointed out, for instance, that he needs new clients for his advertising agency, that there are a lot more top executives on Cape Cod than there are in the wilds of Nova Scotia, and that he might easily meet some exceedingly valuable business contacts there. But you didn't do this. You merely shouted at him, 'We're going to Cape Cod because that's where *I* want to go!' Not a very compelling argument from where *he* sits. Am I right?"

"Yes," she murmured. "You're right."

"The third rule," I went on, "is this: *Create a climate of acquiescence*. It has become a joke, but there's a lot of insight in the old story about the little woman who fetches her husband's pipe and slippers, cooks him a splendid meal, tells him how young and handsome he looks and then asks him for a new car or a fur coat. I don't mean that you have to go in constantly for fulsome praise or insincere flattery. But if you're consistently thoughtful and considerate and just plain nice, your husband is going to love you that much more, and the more he loves you the more he'll be willing to give your wishes priority over his own—at least occasionally. Have you really been working at creating that sort of climate in your home? Or have you and your husband just been arguing about whose whims get preference, like two spoiled children quarreling over a lollipop?"

"I guess I could have worked harder at it," she admitted. She wrinkled her nose defiantly. "But so could Paul!"

I had to laugh. "I'm sure you both could! Now the fourth and last rule in this art of persuasion is *patience*. You can't always expect to have your hopes confirmed or your wishes granted instantly. You have to plant the seed of an idea, and then wait. If you insist on an immediate answer, very often it will be a negative one—because most people don't like to be backed into a corner."

"How can patience help me with this problem?" she wanted to know.

"Well," I said, "let me tell you about the time years ago when Norman and I were thinking of buying a house. We'd been married for thirteen years, but we'd never had one of our own. We'd always lived in city apartments. Now the children were growing up, and we wanted a place where we could see trees and grass and hills around us. We heard of an old farmhouse for sale on Quaker Hill in Pawling, New York, and we went to look at it.

"I fell in love with the house at first sight. It was an old eighteenth-century farmhouse set in about twenty acres of lovely rolling countryside. There was a wide lawn with great stately maples. There were original hinges on some of the doors, wide, hand-hewn floor boards, four fireplaces—with an old brick oven built into the largest one—

and andirons that had supported blazing logs for more than one hundred fifty years...oh, all sorts of marvelous things!

"I was dying to buy that house, but Norman said flatly 'no' and gave all sorts of reasons. We didn't have the money. (This was true, but I knew we could borrow it.) The house was too big; we'd rattle around in it. (This was not so true; three children and some pets can fill up almost any house.) Finally, he said, the neighbor's barn cut off the view. (The barn did cut off some of the view, but not all—and anyway it was a gem of a barn: antique, picturesque, an impressive part of the landscape.)

"I tried to point out some of the features of the house that appealed to me, but Norman was not in a mood for listening. 'I'm sorry,' he said. 'We can't afford it, and I'm all against it, so you'd better forget about it.'

"I was tempted to argue, but I didn't. I didn't because I knew that the frugality built into Norman during his childhood was a very real and powerful thing. He was appalled by the prospect of going heavily into debt. I knew that summoning up the determination to break through that childhood conditioning would take time—and that nothing I could say would hurry the process. So I decided to wait—until the timing was right.

"While I waited, though, I applied the second rule of persuasion: self-interest. I didn't specify *what* place, but I reminded Norman from time to time that he needed a quiet, restful place to think, to write, to plan his speeches and sermons. I said I thought he would work better if he owned a piece of land somewhere. I remember I also got our friend, Lowell Thomas, for whom Norman had great respect and affection, and who also lived in Pawling, to tell him that the barn, with its hand-hewn beams, was one of the finest in the whole state of New York! Which it was.

"I also worked on creating a climate of acquiescence. In a lot of small things I made myself as agreeable and thoughtful as possible. I consciously put Norman's needs ahead of my own. And finally this paid off, because six months later, out of the blue, Norman suddenly said to me, 'Ruth, I know how much you loved that old farmhouse up in Pawling. I've been thinking. Maybe we could get a mortgage and somehow borrow the rest of the money...' "

Young Mrs. Johnson clapped her hands delightedly. "So you got it!"

"Yes," I said, "we got it. We had many happy years there. But you know, I'll confess something to you—my husband never was really reconciled to that barn. And so, almost a quarter of a century later, when another property came on the market not far away, with no barn and a really sensational view, I agreed to sell the house I loved and buy the one without a barn. Why? Because I had had my dream house for a long, long time. I thought it was high time my husband had his view!"

"And by doing that," she said thoughtfully, "you've created a new climate of acquiescence!"

"Well," I said, "I think we've got a kind of permanent one in our house by this time."

"I'm going right home," she said, "and start building one myself. I'll let you know how I come out!"

And she did, too. A few weeks later I got a telegram that said: "Two weeks in Nova Scotia, two on Cape Cod. Everything wonderful, thanks to you and the indispensable art."

She didn't even sign it.

She didn't have to!

Dear Jennie,

This will have to be a short note because a new session of our School of Practical Christianity gets under way here in Pawling today. More than 200 ministers of all denominations and their wives will gather for three days of fellowship and spiritual renewal...and I'm responsible for seeing that it all runs smoothly!

Just a word, then, about the chapter we just read about the art of persuasion. Certainly persuasion is one of the secrets of staying in love because in a successful marriage, not only do you have to work steadily at staying in love with a man, you also have to persuade him to stay in love with you!

If you're no longer sure of Jack's love for you, if you're afraid it may be diminishing or even vanishing, perhaps you should ask yourself – or even ask him – a series of questions, searching questions. Why did he fall in love with you in the first place? What qualities did he see in you that made him want to spend the rest of his life with you? Can he name three or four characteristics that, in his opinion, raised you above all the other girls he might have met or known or dated?

Then you have to ask yourself, with total honesty, whether those qualities and traits are still there. If he fell in love with you because you were fun to be with, because you were cheerful and amusing, because you were so aware of his needs and sensitive to his moods, ask yourself – are you still like that? If he fell in love because you were so careful about your appearance, because you never pouted or sulked, because you could take disappointment cheerfully, because you were thoughtful and kind, ask yourself – are those attributes still there? If not, try to figure out where they've gone and why they've gone and how they can be restored.

Self-appraisal, Jennie. **Honestly appraise your own**

personality. That's secret number nine in this challenging business of staying in love.

In haste,

Ruth

P.S. It's not a one-way street. Jack should try it too!

10

"How Wonderful You Are!"

"If you want a man to keep loving you," my grandmother used to say, "you only have to do one thing—appreciate him, and let him know that you do."

That bit of homespun advice would save a lot of marriages, if more people put it into practice.

Just the other day, for example, an unhappy wife came to Norman, worried because love seemed to be draining out of her marriage. It wasn't that her husband was unfaithful, she said, or drank too much, or was stingy or jealous, or had any of the usual faults. It was just that he never praised her for anything she did, no matter how hard she tried. "It may be his ancestry," she said sadly. "His people came from Sweden. They're a rather solid family; none of them is very good at expressing feelings. But I just can't go on like this. I feel as if something terribly important in me is drying up. If I can't get my husband to understand this, I may have to leave him."

Norman asked the husband to come and see him, and he

did. Sure enough, he was a big, blond, blue-eyed man of Scandinavian parentage. When the situation was explained to him, he became rather defensive. "Why," he said, "this is all a lot of nonsense. I love my wife. She knows I love her. Why should I keep telling her so all the time?"

"This wife of yours," said Norman, "is she a good housekeeper?"

"Sure," said the man. "An excellent housekeeper."

"And a good cook?"

"Yes," said the man. "As a matter of fact, she's a terrific cook."

"When did you last tell her that?" Norman wanted to know.

"I don't remember," said this stubborn Swede. "But why should I tell her something she already knows?"

Now, Norman has a whole kit of psychological tools that he uses in his counseling work: stories, illustrations, quotations from philosophers and wise men, insights from the Bible, sometimes even jokes designed to make a point and hammer it into the listener's head. In this case, he reached into his kit and pulled out his William James illustration.

Norman rates William James, the great psychologist, as one of the finest minds America has ever produced. He told his visitor how James once wrote a book, a profound study of human nature, listing and analyzing all the emotions that motivate and control human behavior. The book was hailed as a masterpiece, but years later James was heard to say ruefully that he had neglected to include the most basic emotion of all. That emotion was the universal craving for recognition, the deep, unwavering desire in every human heart to be appreciated.

"Now tell me," said Norman to the big Swede, "what do you do for a living?"

His visitor said that he was a manufacturer of electrical appliances.

"Are they good appliances?" Norman wanted to know.

The Swede assured him they were the best.

"Does it please you," Norman continued, "when your customers praise your product?"

The man admitted that it did.

"And is this praise a factor in making you want to keep up your standards and do your best?"

The man agreed that this was the case.

"Well," said Norman, "a woman who decorates a house, or cooks and serves a fine meal, or even irons a shirt skillfully is doing something just as creative as you are doing in manufacturing a good appliance. She needs and deserves praise and recognition just as much as you do. You may have a thousand customers, and so you have a thousand potential sources of appreciation. But she has only one—and that is you. Because you have failed to grasp this simple truth, your marriage is in danger. But fortunately there is a simple solution."

"What solution?" asked the man, now quite concerned.

"To begin with," said Norman, "when you go home from work this afternoon, take your wife some flowers."

"Flowers?" cried the Swede. "She'll think I'm suffering from a guilty conscience. She'll ask me what I've been up to!"

"Don't give her a chance to ask questions," Norman said. "Hand her the flowers and say, 'These are for you just because you are you!' "

The man finally agreed to carry out these instructions. The next day the wife called Norman and asked if he had prodded her husband into such unheard-of behavior. Norman just laughed and told her that he and her husband had had a talk, and that maybe this was the beginning of a new relationship. And from what we've heard since, it was.

Appreciation takes a thousand forms. It can be a casual compliment: "My, that's a pretty dress, or an effective hairdo, or a good-looking tie!" It can be an expression of deep affection and closeness: "Darling, I don't know what I'd do without you!" It can be a smile or a simple "Well done!" from a boss to a subordinate. We have a friend, a salesman, who has to travel a great deal. Whenever he goes on a trip, his wife writes a little note and hides it in his suitcase or in one of his pockets, just a line or two, telling him that she loves him, that she will miss him, that she thinks he's wonderful, that she knows the trip will be a success. I remember once he showed one of these notes to Norman and me. It said, "Why don't we make love twice as often?" Now there's a wife with a *real* sense of adventure!

There's no doubt about it: Appreciation in any form at any time brightens anyone's existence, however drab it may be. And like a beam of sunlight striking a mirror, the brightness is reflected right back to you.

One rule I've learned in my own efforts to master the art of appreciation is this: When the impulse comes to say the friendly thing, or do the little kindness that shows appreciation, act on it right away—otherwise it will vanish. Even when you realize how welcome a gesture of appreciation would be, it's terribly easy to put it off—and then forget all about it. I hate to think of the number of times I've thought of writing a note, or making a phone call, or sending a gift to express appreciation—and then failed to follow through.

There's only one answer to this kind of procrastination:

Do it now!

On a trip to Spain, for example, I needed a new evening dress so I ordered one made in Madrid. We were there only briefly, and the seamstresses in the couturier's salon worked overtime to have the dress ready. On the way to my last fitting, the thought crossed my mind that I really should do something to show my gratitude, something a little more tangible than mere verbal thanks. So I stopped the taxi, got out, found a store that sold candy, and bought some to take to the girls who had worked so hard on the dress.

You might have thought I'd brought them a bushel of emeralds! Nobody, apparently, had made such a gesture before. Their appreciation of my appreciation was so evident that I had a warm, good feeling all through my fitting and for the rest of the day.

It's really the old law of the echo in operation: When you send out an impulse of kindness or thoughtfulness, it comes bouncing right back to you. We have a friend, a housewife down in Florida, who always puts out coffee and doughnuts for the men who come to her back door to collect the garbage. She does it, she says, because she thinks they have just about the most thankless, disagreeable, and underpaid job in the whole structure of society. She went away on a vacation recently, and so the coffee breaks ended temporarily. But when she got back, all the garbage men climbed off their truck, came to the door, took off their gloves and solemnly shook her hand, asking about her trip and behaving like old friends. "We missed you," one of them said to her, "not because of the coffee, but because you really care about people!" She treasured that compliment as if it came from a prime minister—and she should have.

Every day every wife and husband should take a long, careful look at their married partner, decide what traits are most admirable, and seek out ways of expressing that admiration. In our marriage, for example, I try to appreciate how enormously difficult it is to create and deliver, week after week, year after year, sermons and speeches that will interest and inspire and help people. I remind myself how much effort and discipline—and sometimes discouragement—go into that kind of lonely task, a task that demands the very best that you've got to give, a task that no one else can ever do for you. I never cease to be amazed at the standards my husband sets for himself and the efforts he makes to live up to those standards.

I try to show my appreciation for this and for many other things by letting him know how much I admire his dedication, by praising him for his sermons or his speeches, by trying to shield him from unnecessary distractions and interruptions and worries. Conversely, he is generous in telling me how helpful I am to him, how much he depends on me, how grateful he is for a home where things run smoothly and where his energies are not siphoned off into petty distractions or details.

Not that we spend all our time doing this! Obviously, there's a line that divides sincere appreciation from overeffusiveness or calculated flattery. But I'm sure that for every person who oversteps the line, there are ten thousand who never even approach it.

That's why most of us need to make a conscious effort to be more appreciative of our marriage partners. Is your husband a commuter? Give some thought to the long, uncomfortable hours he spends getting to and from his job. Take this into consideration when he gets home. Don't burden him with a lot of household problems the moment he steps off the bus or the train.

Does your wife have a job? Don't expect her to bring home a paycheck and also cope with all the housekeeping tasks by herself. Show your appreciation of her financial contribution by helping her with the dishes regularly as well as other household tasks. You may be an executive in the office, but she's an executive in the home. A woman who runs a household, buying the groceries, cooking the meals, doing the laundry, coping with the children, making decisions about a thousand different details all day long, is just as much an executive as any businessman—maybe even more.

Simply showing interest in another person's activities can be a form of appreciation. It helps when someone asks: "How did your day go? What happened at the office? What did your women's club discuss this afternoon?" Routine questions? Certainly. And yet they make the other person feel that you're interested in what he does, that you want to share his burdens and his triumphs—that you care.

One family we know keeps their appreciation-level high with a sort of dinner-table game that they've worked out over the years. The father usually starts it by asking, "What was the most interesting thing that happened to you today?" (Or the funniest, or the most unexpected, or the most annoying—any superlative will do.) Then each member of the family responds in turn. Sometimes the father will ask, "What single thing in your life are you most grateful for right now?" The five-year-old may be grateful for her kitten. The ten-year-old may be grateful for his bicycle. The teen-ager may be grateful because his school's football team has won a game. The whole idea is to strengthen a sense of appreciation and encourage the expression of it.

Once, I remember, when we were visiting this particular

family, we came down to breakfast on a bleak, rainy morning. "Well," said the father when we were all seated at the breakfast table, "this day looks a little dreary, I'll admit. But there must be some good things about it. Let's each try to name one good thing about this day."

So around the table they went. One of the children thought that the rain would make the farmers happy. Another said she liked the sound the raindrops made on the roof. A third said gravely that the day must be a good day because God had made it the way it was. The father said that it was a good day because they had good friends visiting them. Then it was the mother's turn. "It's a good day," she said, "because we're all together." She smiled at her husband. "But the best thing about this day, or any day," she said to him, "is you."

Expressed affection...the best of all methods to use when you want to light a glow in somebody's heart, and feel the warmth of it in your own.

Dear Jennie,

What fun it is for a writer to reread something she has written and be able to say to herself, "Yes, that's it. That's what I was trying to say, and I don't have anything to add to it." I know it sounds a bit smug, but that's the way I feel about the chapter we've read this past week.

I think William James was absolutely right when he said that the hunger for recognition is one of the deepest of human emotions. Yet, strangely, it's a yearning that often goes unfulfilled inside the framework of marriage. Even people who are still in love can make the mistake of assuming that their partner doesn't need to be reminded of their affection, their admiration, their loyalty or their love. And almost always this assumption is completely wrong.

A writer friend said to me the other day, "To be openly loved, to be manifestly admired, these are human needs as basic as breathing. Why, then, needing them so much ourselves, do we deny them so often to others?"

This is a good question for every married person to ponder, Jennie.

So there you have the tenth secret of staying in love. Paste it up on your dressing table mirror. Better still, engrave it on your mind and heart.

Appreciate your mate.

With love,

Ruth

11

When The Sparks Fly

EVERY minister's wife—and every minister too—knows that a lot of people tend to become solemn and pious when the preacher comes around. Everybody is suddenly on his best behavior. Everybody puts his best foot forward, with the result that at times nothing seems quite real!

Countless times, talking with a married couple I've just met, I've had them say to me, "Oh, yes, we've been married fifteen years (or twenty, or thirty) and we've never had a cross word between us." I always smile and nod happily, but what I'm really thinking is, "How dull! How boring! What a drag a marriage like that would be!"

I certainly don't want to imply that a bitter quarrel in marriage is a good thing. People say and do things in anger that can damage any relationship—sometimes permanently. But I do think that a disagreement between married partners can actually be constructive and useful if (and it's a big "if") it's handled in the right way.

Over the years, there have been plenty of areas where Norman and I were not in accord. There still are. I wouldn't think of agreeing with him on every subject! But we have learned certain do's and don'ts that tend to turn potential arguments into useful discussions.

One, for example, is the importance of easing up gradually on an area of disagreement, taking just a piece of it at first (the least explosive piece), discussing that aspect, then letting the matter rest for a while. We've found that if you nibble around the edges of an argument, instead of trying to bite off more than either of you can chew, you're likely to be able to digest the problem much better in the end. I heard a very successful business executive say once that when a touchy subject has to be dealt with in his board room, he tries to make sure that the discussion is conducted in slow motion. That's a pretty good rule for marital discussions, too.

Another technique that I have learned to value is simply the practice of silence at certain times. There are areas in arguments—and every married person recognizes them—where you suddenly realize that your partner is no longer talking about the issue at hand, but about something else that is highly charged with emotion. When this happens, the best thing to do is not to argue or counterpunch, but just let the other person talk himself out. As the old saying goes, "Silence is golden."

There are various other common-sense things that can take the sting out of marital disagreement if you can just keep them in mind: the importance of *compromise* (compromise doesn't mean giving in); the value of *emphasizing the positive* when making your case (negative arguments rarely influence anybody); the trick of trying—*really* trying—to *put yourself in your adversary's shoes* and seeing the issue from his point of view. All these guidelines are helpful, but it's surprising how many married people have never thought of them or tried to apply them. When disagreements arise, they just react with anger—and react again with more anger.

When young wives seek my advice in such matters, as they do quite frequently, I'm always amused at their assumption that, being a minister's wife, I have never heard an angry or unkind word from my husband and consequently don't know what a real husband-wife altercation is. It's true that Norman and I almost never have any serious differences nowadays, but this was not always the case. When we were first married, Norman was a young man in a very demanding job. There were times when he wondered if he was equal to the job (he was more than equal to it, but he had a kind of basic insecurity that made him worry anyway), and when the tension caused by this reached a certain point, he could be very hard to live with.

All wives, to some extent, have to act as lightning rods, but this is not the most pleasant role in the world, and in those days I wasn't mature enough for it. So when Norman was short-tempered or irritable, I had a tendency to flare up in return, or else react with hurt feelings. When he was sarcastic—and being a master of words he could put a real sting into them—I would often try to strike back. But when I did, he would remember what I had said in anger and use my own words against me. Verbally, I was no match for him.

The main lesson I learned from all this was that if I wanted the battle or the black mood to end quickly, I had to control myself. If I cut off the fuel by refusing to become angry or fight back, the whole thing blew over much more quickly.

Fortunately for me, there was a fundamental streak of fairness in Norman that made him capable of admitting his own failing now and then. I remember one time when he was being his most objectionable self. I stood it as long as I could. Then I took him into our bedroom and closed the door so that the children couldn't hear me and really told him off. "For once," I said furiously, "you are going to keep still and listen to me. You're being mean and hateful, and you know it. Those black moods of yours are your worst character defect, and yet you won't face up to this or try to change it!" I ranted and raved.

Usually in such a situation he would deny my accusations or defend his position, but now he simply said, "You're right. I know I need to work on that."

From that moment on, he seemed to see himself in a different light. He didn't turn into a paragon overnight, but he was certainly easier to live with!

I think that in many marriages the first long step toward happiness comes with the realization that *everyone* has some unpleasant quirk or weakness, and that an important part of marriage consists in trying to balance or compensate for such eccentricities or failings in the person you're sharing your life with.

For example, I know one wife whose husband is a compulsive spender. He throws money around, partly because he's a generous person, partly because he is somewhat insecure. He wants people to like him and thinks that they will if he always picks up the check. He can't afford this kind of extravagance, but he can't seem to help it.

The wife knows that she can't oppose this tendency in her husband directly; she has tried and failed. And so she opposes it indirectly. She avoids restaurant gatherings, saying she prefers to eat at home. If she and her husband go to a baseball game or to the movies with another couple, she will often give the other wife the money for her own and her husband's ticket in advance, thus heading off any grand gesture on her husband's part. He teases her good-naturedly about being a tightwad, but everyone who knows them is aware that she is simply protecting their marriage and their life together—and in so doing is performing the basic function of a loving wife.

Most young wives will find, as they grow older and wiser, that they can almost never change objectionable or undesirable characteristics in their husbands by frontal assault. Angry recriminations just make matters worse. The only approach that works is rational discussions in moments of calmness, appeals to fair-mindedness, or quiet demonstrations of how hurtful or unwise the objectionable quality really is.

I knew one young wife—I'll call her Mrs. Harrison—who married into a very close-knit family. They were not only very fond of one another, they were all great talkers. Whenever there was a family gathering, this combination of affection and fluency became overwhelming. Nobody else could get a word in edgewise. Guests just had to sit there, mute and helpless. The members of the family were so interested in one another, and in family activities, anecdotes, jokes, and reminiscences, that the rest of the world and the people in it didn't exist for them.

Some new wives might have accepted this situation with resignation. Some might have smouldered in silence. But this was a forthright girl, so she decided to take it up with her husband. "Darling," she said (always a good word to begin a discussion with!), "I don't think any of you realize it, but when you Harrisons get together you're really quite rude. You don't show even polite interest in what anyone outside the family might have to say. You just turn them off."

"Oh, come now," the husband said, "you're being hypersensitive, aren't you? You know perfectly well we're always delighted to hear anything you have to say. All you have to do is speak up!"

"I do try to speak up," she told him. "And I've heard other people try. But it's hopeless. If we attempt to tell a story, one of you always tops it with one of your own. Or else it reminds you of some family episode that you just have to tell about. And the worst of it is that you're not even aware that you're doing it!"

"I still think you're exaggerating," her husband said cheerfully. "We can't be as bad as all that."

The young wife said no more, but she went out and rented a battery-powered tape recorder. At the next family gathering she hid the machine in one of the compartments of the sideboard and recorded the whole dinner-table conversation. That night, when she and her husband were alone, she played the tape, stopping it occasionally to insert her own comments. ("Now here's Jim's wife trying feebly to talk about her own college days; notice how your mother cuts her off." Or, "This is me, trying to speak up the way you told me I should. See how far I get!")

The husband, utterly amazed, called a family conference of his parents and brothers and sisters and played the tape for them, adding some of the comments his wife had made. Everyone was astounded. Fortunately, being a warmhearted as well as a conversation-monopolizing group, they took no offense but honestly tried to mend their ways and succeeded, as my friend said dryly, "part of the time, anyway."

Sometimes a sharp quarrel that clears the air is better than a sullen deadlock that drags on and on. And I have known of cases where a married pair quarreled so violently and hit bottom so hard that they were shaken into a new and better relationship.

There was a couple in Florida, typical young-marrieds, who had this experience. Their troubles began when the husband received a promotion and they moved into a suburb where the residents considered themselves the local jet set. The young pair stopped going to church, because none of their new friends went to church. They started to drink more than was good for them. They began to quarrel and bicker about trifles. Their marriage was drifting toward the rocks.

One night at a country-club dance where everyone had been drinking heavily, a man who had recently been divorced began to make obvious advances to the young wife. It seemed to the husband that, far from discouraging these advances, his wife actually welcomed them and led the man on. He dragged her from the party, and flung her into their car and drove home, berating her bitterly. She replied in kind. By the time they reached their house, they were both wild with anger. As they got out of the car in their garage, the wife said something so infuriating that her husband lost all self-control and struck her, knocking her to the concrete floor.

She lay there, crumpled like a broken flower, a trickle of blood running down her chin. The man stared down at her, horrified, all the anger draining out of him. He fell on his knees and gathered her in his arms. "Oh, God," he cried. "God help us!"

"Yes," the wife said brokenly, "we need Him to help us. We need to get back to Him before it's too late." Clinging together they sobbed and prayed. And because in this extremity they had someone to turn to, someone all-powerful and all-compassionate, they were able to climb out of the pit they had dug for themselves and become friends and lovers once more.

Friends and lovers—when that balance is achieved in marriage, and survives all the storms and stresses, nothing in the world brings so much happiness and so much joy.

Dear Jennie,

It's a pleasant irony to report that I have been rereading the chapter on quarreling couples in one of the most peaceful environments in the world, the beautiful island of Maui out here in the sun-drenched Hawaiian Islands: Norman was asked to speak to a convention here. So many people came that they asked him to give two talks, a week apart. So here we are, for once, with a little time on our hands, a little time to ourselves, and we are enjoying it tremendously.

This means that I can write you a more leisurely letter, and I thought I'd try to give you a glimpse of a problem that came to our attention shortly before we left the mainland. The problem involved a faltering marriage, not unlike your own in some ways. But the deterioration had gone further than in your case. We had tried once or twice to offer advice to this couple, whom we knew quite well, but apparently it did no good because a few days before we were to leave on this trip we heard that the husband had left home and moved to a hotel.

When Norman heard this, he became quite vehement as he sometimes does when we discuss such a situation. "Nothing good can come of this," he said. "If a man leaves his wife, or vice versa, a basic law is being broken. I'm not talking about civil law or man-made law. I'm talking about a law of the universe, a law of God. The Bible says that God created the human race in two forms: 'male and female created He them.' He endowed the male with certain attributes and the female with complementary attributes. Balanced opposites, you might say. Like night and day. Or summer and winter. Or light and darkness. These things are eternal. They're not meant to be changed or tampered with, because God made them and He knew what He was doing."

By now Norman was pacing up and down the way he does when something really agitates him. "A man by himself may have strength and determination and aggressiveness, but he's not complete. A woman may have great sensitivity and intuition and feminine insights, but she's not complete either. These incomplete units are designed to become one unit, to fit together like pieces of a jigsaw puzzle. That's what the Bible means when it talks about the twain becoming one flesh – that is, one person. One complete person. The man and the woman need to join their hearts and minds and skills and bodies, fuse them into a single organism that has more than twice the strength and twice the wisdom and twice the love capacity of either of them separately. Why can't people see this and understand it? It's so obvious! Love may begin with biological attraction – that's been built into us too, but that attraction should lead to the kind of fusion I'm talking about. That's what marriage is – or should be. A fusion of opposites that is in harmony with divine law."

"My goodness," I said to Norman, "I wish those friends of ours could hear you now!"

"I do too!" said Norman. "Let's get them in here one more time and try to talk some sense into them."

Well, Norman did ask them to come to see us, and after some hesitation they did. Each of them had the air of wary defiance that we've seen so often in couples who are falling out of love. It's an attitude (the Bible has a word for it: pride) that makes compromise or sharing the blame almost impossible.

But Norman has a wonderful way of dealing with these tangled situations. Some marvelous psychic radar tells him when to be patient, when to be gentle, when to be tough. He put the two adversaries into comfortable chairs facing his desk. I sat over on the sofa, ready either to listen or to try to be helpful if I were asked.

Norman began by telling them an amusing story of a mishap we had had recently. It was so absurd – he always pokes fun at himself–that both of our visitors had to laugh, and I could see the wife's clenched hands relax a little in her lap.

"Now," said Norman, "let's get down to business. We all know why we're here. Ruth and I are very fond of both of you. We don't like seeing you unhappy. So let's try a little even-handed experiment." He held up both hands, palms outward, fingers separated. "Eleanor, let's start with you. I want you to tell me the five chief weaknesses or deficiencies in this man that are preventing you from having a happy relationship with him. Take your time. Think before you say anything. We're in no hurry."

"I'm not sure," said Eleanor a bit grimly, "that I can limit it to five!"

"Five is all you get," Norman said firmly. "I have only five fingers on each hand."

So Eleanor gave us her catalogue of grievances. Then Don did the same thing. The complaints all had a very human ring. Discouraging though it sounded, I felt each was telling the truth about the other. I noticed that Norman was making notes as they talked.

"Well," said Norman when they were through, "each of you seems to have made quite a study of the failings and shortcomings of the other. That's not such a bad thing, because we all have weaknesses and it helps to know what they are. I think the trouble in your case is that each of you regards those weaknesses in the other person as threats or as annoyances rather than as opportunities–which is what they really are.

"Eleanor, you say Don drinks too much. Is that a weakness? Of course it is! But why does he drink too much? One reason may be a fear that he's not quite up to the demands of his job and liquor gives him a false sense of security. Or there may be some other area where he feels inadequate. Isn't it a wife's role to locate that area and give support and encouragement and understanding—in other words, fill the gap caused by the weakness? Wouldn't you get enormous satisfaction out of that?

"Don, you say Eleanor is too possessive and unreasonably jealous. Are those weaknesses? Sure they are. But they come from insecurity, from fear that she will lose you, or not be able to keep up with you, or somehow be left behind. Instead of telling yourself constantly how annoying that is, why don't you look at it as a challenge, a problem that you can solve by being more attentive and more reassuring? If she felt sure of your love, she wouldn't clutch at it so desperately. Is that so hard to understand?"

Norman went on through the remaining category of grievances, showing how each partner could compensate for or help to correct the shortcomings of the other. Then he repeated to them what he had said to me about male and female being divinely designed to complement each other. I could see that both of our visitors were deeply impressed. Eleanor had tears in her eyes and Don sat with his head bowed, listening.

"Now," said Norman, "let's have a prayer about this. I know you loved each other once, and I believe you love each other still. The Lord brought you together, and He wants you together, so let's ask Him to help you make a new start."

We had a prayer and they went out together. And something in me felt that they are going to stay together from now on.

Would this sort of approach help with your problems, Jennie? Why don't you and Jack take a fresh look at yourselves? Stop thinking of yourselves as obstinate squares and circles that don't overlap. Think of yourselves as pieces of a beautifully made jigsaw puzzle, each quite different, but each designed by God Himself to fit together so closely and so snugly that not even the cracks are visible.

So, I think secret number eleven is like the jigsaw concept. It is: **Blend your lives together**.

Your friend,

Ruth

12

The Healing Art Of Absorption

SOMETIMES I think the best epitaph a wife could hope for would be just six words: "She was a wonderful shock absorber." Carved on a headstone, that might not look very elegant or very spiritual, I know. But to go through life cushioning shocks or blows for other people calls for a set of characteristics very close to the Christian ideal. It calls for selflessness, service, compassion, and kindness—just as religion does.

Being a shock absorber comes easily to a mother, because it's reinforced by instinct. Your toddler falls and bangs his forehead; your second-grader burns her fingers on a hot stove; your teen-ager is in tears because her feelings have been hurt by some thoughtless friend. Here the protective instinct is swift and sure: you dry the tears, you say the consoling or comforting thing, you put the right medicine—physically or emotionally—on the hurt.

But it's more difficult for husbands and wives to respond so automatically to each other's needs. Here two adults are involved, two separate and sometimes demanding egos. In dozens of marriage situations, affection whispers: "This is my man (or woman). I love him. Therefore I will try to spare him and protect him." But there is also a contrary voice, a churlish sort of voice that grumbles: "Well, he's a grown man, isn't he? He ought to be able to cope with his own problems. Besides, I've got my own difficulties...and what's he doing to help me?"

In other words, where marriage is concerned, no one is a natural, ready-made shock absorber. It's an art—and you have to learn it, just the way you learn any other skill or art.

What does it take to learn it? It takes intelligence, discipline, practice at anticipating trouble, adroitness at moving to head it off or minimize it. Above all, it takes motivation. You have to be able to see clearly that the more you can spare or shield your marriage partner, the stronger and deeper will be his gratitude and his affection for you.

It doesn't matter whether your husband is a bus driver or the president of the United States, there are always ways in which a wife can ease the burden, reduce the tension, eliminate unnecessary worry.

Speaking of bus drivers, let me tell you about two good friends of ours. Fred and Betty are strong Christians, good citizens, the salt of the earth. Fred is a New York City bus driver. He is a sensitive, high-strung person. But he didn't always think highly of himself; in fact, he thought he was a failure. He looked upon bus driving as an unimportant task. But he had been at it for so long that changing jobs would have been difficult. He wasn't really trained for anything else.

This sense of personal inadequacy kept gnawing away at Fred until one day his wife could stand it no longer. She sought out Norman and me and asked, "What on earth can I do to bring happiness into Fred's mind? What can I do to make him feel that his job is important? I'm convinced that it is. He helps people who ride in his bus by being cheerful and patient and friendly. He watches older people and young children to see that they don't get into trouble. But still he feels inferior. Do you think you could possibly talk to him? He doesn't really listen to me."

We said we would, and Norman did talk to Fred. "I tried," he told us later, "to make him see that if you're serving people—which he is—you're serving God. And if you're serving God, one form of service is as honorable and worthwhile as another."

"Did you get through to him?" I asked.

Norman shook his head doubtfully. "I don't know. He agreed with everything I said. But I had the feeling that he was just being polite. I also had the feeling that until Fred is able to straighten up and look people in the eye with pride and confidence and *say* he's a bus driver, he'll never be at peace with himself."

"I'm afraid you're right," I said.

Fred was an expert driver of any kind of car, and quite often he would offer to drive us to a dinner or a speaking engagement out of town. This suited me fine, because Norman never liked to drive when he had a speech on his mind, and I found it easier and more pleasant to relax with him instead of battling with the traffic myself. On these expeditions, Betty usually joined us, and the four of us always had a fine time riding out and riding back.

One rainy night Fred and Betty drove us out to a country club in New Jersey where Norman was to be the after-dinner speaker. It was quite an elaborate affair, with important men and women from all over the state—politicians, business tycoons, high-ranking military people, and so on. Fred and Betty had planned to go to a restaurant for dinner, and then come back for us. But on this occasion, at the last minute, two guests were unable to come, and Norman asked the host if the two friends who had driven us out from the city could take their places.

The host was very gracious and said he'd be delighted. But Fred hesitated. When we kept urging him, he mumbled, "I'm just a bus driver. I don't belong with those people in there."

Then up spoke Betty, lovingly but firmly. "Fred," she said, "you're my husband, and I love you, and I'm proud of you, and as long as I feel that way I don't see any reason in the world why we couldn't accept these good people's invitation."

Fred looked at her for about half a minute without a word. "All right," he said finally, "if that's the way you feel, we'll do it."

They took the two seats at our table and everything seemed to be going fine until suddenly, in one of those unexpected lulls that always seem to happen at dinner parties, I heard a man across the table from Fred—he was an international banker, a very prominent man—say, "And what line of business are you in, sir?"

I held my breath, because the whole table seemed to be listening, and I knew Betty was holding hers, too. Then all of a sudden Fred smiled a friendly, relaxed smile. "I drive a bus," he said. He said it loud and clear, but the banker was so taken aback that he evidently thought he hadn't heard Fred correctly. "You do *what*?" he said incredulously.

Fred gave Betty just the flicker of a grin, and then looked across the table at the banker. "I drive a bus in New York City," he said. "I'm a bus driver."

"Well, my goodness," said the banker, "that's marvelous! I've always envied the job you fellows do. Tell me, don't you ever lose your temper with all that traffic and all those people pushing and shoving?"

He wasn't being condescending or merely polite. His interest was completely genuine. And that was only the first question. Other guests joined in with real interest, real curiosity. And suddenly there was Fred the bus driver talking easily and naturally about his work with no hesitancy, no apology, no sense of inferiority. Norman looked at me and I looked at Norman and I think we both said a little prayer of thanksgiving. Because faith had worked a small miracle, as it so often does—and the faith that did it was Betty's.

Sooner or later in most marriages a situation is likely to arise in which one partner is threatened, upset, driven to extreme action that may or may not be wise. And this is precisely the time when the other partner can salvage or retrieve the situation by keeping calm, praying for guidance, and above all by taking some of the shock—absorbing it—until the worst of the crisis is over.

I remember very well the time in a midwestern city when we were staying in a very large hotel, one of the key properties in a very important hotel chain. We had stayed there before, and had become friendly with the assistant manager and his wife, both admirable people. On this occasion we got a telephone call from this man asking us to have lunch with him and his wife, saying they would like to talk to us. It was a personal matter, he said—and to them an important one.

I'll never forget how they looked when they came into the dining room. The man was pale, tense, obviously much upset. The woman was upset, too, but I could see that her whole concern was for her husband. She was not thinking about herself.

What had happened, it seemed, was the manager of the

hotel was retiring. This had been expected for some time, and the assistant manager had hoped that the job would be his. He had practically been told as much, he said, by a high official of the hotel chain. But that very morning word had come down that a manager was to be brought in from outside. Our friend was not to get the job after all. He was so disappointed, hurt, and angry, that he had decided to resign. He had been on the point of calling up his superiors and telling them just what he thought of them when his wife remembered that we were in the hotel. She had persuaded him to talk to us first.

Now, if anything, the wife was angrier than her husband. She loved him, believed in him, hated to see him hurt. Her first instinct, I'm sure, was to strike out at the thing that was hurting him—which in this case was the impersonal management of a great hotel chain.

But she also knew that at the moment her husband's judgment was impaired, that he was capable of doing something he might regret later. Also, the practical, sensible homemaker inside the angry wife knew that she and her husband were both middle-aged, that jobs as good as the one they had did not grow on trees, that they had two children to think about—one in college. She knew her man well enough to know that in his present state of mind nothing she could say would have much effect. But she also knew that he admired Norman and might listen to him. So here they were.

In a case like this, Norman never says much at first. He always encourages the person in trouble to pour it out, ventilate all the anger, the frustration, the bitterness, whatever (as he puts it) is "heating up the mind." So the assistant manager talked for some time, reviewing all his past contributions to the hotel, marshaling all the arguments why he was perfectly capable of taking over the top job, occasionally appealing to his wife for reconfirmation—which she always gave.

Finally, when he had talked himself out, Norman began to place "cool" ideas in the vacancies left by all the "hot" ones that had come sizzling out of the man. He started out by saying calmly that while this disappointment was hard to take, maybe God had some plan in mind for both of them and that this could be a part of that plan. He said he thought it would be very foolish, though understandable, for the man to quit his job in a fit of anger. "The work you do here is important," Norman said. "You make tired people comfortable. You make dispirited people cheerful. You're a warm, welcoming sort of person. People sense that, and they like it. I think you're in the business God meant you to be in, even if the rung of the ladder you want is still out of reach."

The man stared at the tablecloth and said nothing, but I could see that he was listening.

"Now," said Norman, "you are an intelligent person and a big person, so I am going to make a suggestion that a small person or a stupid person could not follow. I suggest that you make yourself swallow your injured pride and your sense of injustice and treat the new manager with great courtesy and respect. As you know better than anyone, you can make his new assignment hard, or you can make it easy. I hope you will make it easy by cheerfully helping him in every way. After all, he hasn't done anything unfair. I don't think you should focus your resentment on him."

Then he turned to his wife. "And I have the same suggestion for you. Treat the new manager's wife as nicely as you possibly can. After all, she's in a difficult position too. Everyone will know that you hoped the job would go to your husband. Everyone will be watching for you to show resentment or hostility. Don't give them that satisfaction. Treat the new boss just the way you'd want him to treat you, if you were in his shoes."

I remember how the assistant made a wry face and gave a reluctant laugh. "I can see we made a mistake inviting you two to have lunch with us," he said. "You're telling us to act like Christians. And that's just the way we don't feel like acting."

Norman and I laughed, too, because we knew we had gotten through to him. Oh, he still took some convincing. But his wife swung around to our side (she had been there all along, really) and began to point out various ways in which he could be of enormous value to the new man. "You'll be a lot more important to him," she said, "than you were to our old boss, who knew all the ropes. I'll bet you'll have more responsibility, more authority than you've ever had before."

Which is exactly the way things worked out. The new manager was so grateful and so impressed that three years later, when he moved on to yet another job, he recommended our friend so highly that he moved into the top spot with no trouble at all.

There was a kind of postscript to the story, too. Norman happened to meet a man who was on the board of that hotel chain. The talk came around to our friend. "You know," the board member said, "the reason we didn't promote him the first time was that we weren't quite sure how he could handle himself under pressure. We were always afraid that in a tough situation he might let his emotions run away with him. But when he took that disappointment with so much grace and self-control. We decided we must be wrong about him." Then he gave Norman a suspicious look. "You didn't have anything to do with all that, did you?"

"His wife was the key," said Norman cheerfully. "She deserves the credit."

And of course, truly she did!

Dear Jennie,

As I have said, it seems to me that although all of the principles in this book are important, some are more important than others. The chapter on the healing art of absorption contains one of the very most important secrets of all.

The twelfth secret of staying in love is simply this: **Learn to be an effective shock absorber.**

By this I mean to encourage your husband when he is down. Learn to balance his moods of depression or discouragement with hope. Learn to reduce the tension, disappointment, and friction in marriage by taking the light-hearted view.

Your husband needs to know that he can count on you to encourage him and help him through his problems. Be there for him, Jennie. Let him know that you are with him no matter what. Cushion his falls with love. If you can do this, you will truly have a happier husband and a happier marriage.

With love,

Ruth

13

Just For Fun

A Very Short Play in Two Acts

Cast of characters: WELL-KNOWN PREACHER and WIFE
Place: Interlaken, Switzerland. A balcony on the Hotel Victoria-Jungfrau
Time: Ten o'clock on a warm summer morning

ACT I

WELL-KNOWN PREACHER *(gazing pensively at the Jungfrau, which happens to be obscured by clouds)*: "You know, I have an idea. But I'd better not tell you what it is, because you wouldn't approve."

Expectant silence. Wife, who is knitting, says nothing.

WELL-KNOWN PREACHER: "Did you hear me? I said I had an excellent idea. But I'd better not tell you about it, because it would just upset you."

Wife knits on placidly.

WELL-KNOWN PREACHER: "Do you think I ought to tell you? Or would you rather remain happy and undisturbed?"

WIFE *(calmly)*: "Whatever you think best, dear." *(She puts away her knitting.)* "I think the sun is going to come out. Why don't we go for a walk around the meadow?"

WELL-KNOWN PREACHER *(wistfully)*: "Don't you want to know what my idea is?"

WIFE: "Certainly. But only when you're ready to tell me. Oh, look you can see the mountain now. Come on, let's walk."

ACT II

It is thirteen hours later. The well-known preacher and wife are getting ready for bed.

WELL-KNOWN PREACHER: "You know, I think I'd better tell you about the idea I had after all. It will upset you, because it involves changing plans, and I know how you hate changing plans once they're made. But I've been thinking. Instead of going to Hamburg as our itinerary calls for, and shipping the car home from there with all that bother and red tape, why don't we drive back to Stuttgart where we got it and let the manufacturer worry about shipping the car? We could fly home from there. It really makes a lot more sense, don't you think?"

WIFE *(cheerfully)*: "Yes, I do."

WELL-KNOWN PREACHER *(incredulously)*: "You mean, you're not upset?"

WIFE: "Why, no. Not at all."

WELL-KNOWN PREACHER: "Well, that's fine. I was afraid you would be. Are you *sure* you're not?"

WIFE: "Quite sure."

WELL-KNOWN PREACHER: "Well, that's great. Because if you had been upset, then I'd have been upset. It's all settled then. We'll go to Stuttgart, not Hamburg, right?"

WIFE: "Right."

They climb into bed, switch out the lights. Silence. But not for long.

WELL-KNOWN PREACHER: "Ruth, are you sure this change of plans doesn't bother you?"

WIFE: "Quite sure."

WELL-KNOWN PREACHER: "Positive?"

WIFE: "Positive!"

Long pause.

WELL-KNOWN PREACHER: "But *why* aren't you upset?"

WIFE: "Well, dear, I don't want to depress you, but that idea wasn't exactly new."

WELL-KNOWN PREACHER: "It wasn't?"

WIFE: "No, it wasn't. It's exactly what I suggested to you three weeks ago in New York."

WELL-KNOWN PREACHER *(weakly)*: "You did?"

WIFE: "Yes, I did. We were sitting in the kitchen at the Hill Farm, and we were planning this trip, and I said we ought to have the car shipped home from Stuttgart and then fly from there. But you said you wanted to go to Hamburg."

WELL-KNOWN PREACHER *(amazed)*: "I did?"

WIFE: "Yes, you did. Don't you remember?"

WELL-KNOWN PREACHER: "Well, now that you mention it, I do seem to recall some sort of discussion along those lines."

WIFE: "It's still a good idea. There's nothing wrong with having it twice."

Silence. Finally...

WIFE: "Good night, dear."

WELL-KNOWN PREACHER *(in small voice)*: "Good night."

Dear Jennie,

I hope you enjoyed the chapter we read this past week. It was refreshing to me, as well as amusing. Now and then, Norman and I like to poke fun at each other in a gentle, affectionate way like that.

When I wrote that little two-act play, I was teasing Norman about his tendency to change his mind. I was also teasing myself about the way I handle those situations. I read it to Norman the other night, and we found ourselves laughing—the warm, companionable laughter of married people who are also best friends.

They say that the family that prays together stays together. We have already discussed the importance of prayer in marriage. But when it comes to mending cracks between a husband and wife, it's hard to beat shared laughter.

So this is secret number thirteen, Jennie: **Learn to laugh together**. Use this secret whenever possible and it will make your marriage stronger.

Ruth

14

Your Husband's Best Business Consultant—You

ONE complaint that I hear all the time from discontented wives is that their husbands are too wrapped up in business affairs to pay much attention to them. "My husband comes home every night from the office with a briefcase full of papers. All he does is work. I might as well not be there." Or, "My husband is always going on business trips without me. Sometimes I feel more like a widow than a wife."

To such wives I often feel like saying, "If his work is the most important thing in your husband's life, learn to take an interest in it. Urge him to talk to you about it. Instead of resenting it, try to be a part of it."

I'm sure the instant reaction of some women would be: "But I have no business background, no specialized knowledge of my husband's job."

To this I would reply. "That doesn't matter. What you do have is specialized knowledge of your husband himself. You know—or should know—how he reacts to things, whether he tends to be too optimistic or too pessimistic, whether he's too bold or too timid, whether he resents authority or welcomes it, whether he's steady or panicky in a tense situation.

"Very often all you have to do to help him is *listen* intelligently when he talks about his work. Most men have a desperate need for someone in whom they can confide with complete assurance and absolute trust. Many jobs, especially jobs in big corporations, are so fiercely competitive that very often there is no such person in a man's working world. If, as a wife, you can be an always-trustworthy, always-available sounding board, you'll be making an enormous contribution to your husband's career."

A woman may also find, if she forces herself to take an interest in her husband's work, that she has more aptitude for business than she thinks. It never occurred to me, before I was married, that I would end up handling all the financial and tax matters in our family. But it soon became apparent to me that if Norman tried to balance checkbooks or started worrying about mortgages or domestic money matters, his creativity would simply dry up. I took over these chores, at first, mainly to relieve him of this burden. But then I found that I really enjoyed working with figures and budgets and so on. It was fun to use all the training in mathematics that I had had in school and college. What was a nightmare to Norman became a source of satisfaction to me.

Sometimes a woman who makes such an effort will develop into a real executive. Norman and I once had a friend named Charles Ulrich Bay, a very wealthy oilman and shipowner who at one time was the American ambassador to Norway. He also owned the well-known financial firm of Kidder, Peabody, & Co. His wife Josephine was a clear-minded, intelligent woman—and her tycoon husband used her constantly as a sounding board. "Here's a business proposition that seems pretty good to me," he'd say to her. "Now, I want you to argue against it. Tell me what's wrong with it. Poke holes in it. Play the devil's advocate. Go ahead. Convince me that it's no good."

"But I don't know enough about it," Josephine would object.

"Telephone the office," he would retort. "Have them send you all the facts, all the statistics, all the reports. Learn everything you can about it today, and we'll discuss it again tonight."

For years this challenging give-and-take went on. Then Mr. Bay died. Norman was asked to conduct the funeral and he did. We rode back from Woodlawn Cemetery in the car with the widow. She was bearing up bravely, but did not try to hide the depth of her grief or the extent of her loss. "I don't know how I'm going to live without him," she kept saying. "I just don't know what I'm going to do."

"Josephine," Norman said gently, "I know what Rick would want you to do. He'd want you to take over his work, take charge of everything yourself. Don't you realize that all these years he's been training you to do just that? Nobody knows as much about all his enterprises as you do. If ever a man taught his wife how to get along without him, he did."

"Do you really believe," she said slowly, "that I have what it takes to step into his shoes?"

"I believe it," Norman said. "What's more, your husband believed it. So why don't you make up your mind to do it—and do it!"

Josephine Bay did make up her mind, and she did do it. She became the first woman president of the big financial house of Kidder, Peabody, & Co., and president of the American Export Lines. She became, in the opinion of many experts, the greatest businesswoman in the United States. And it all began during those quiet hours in her own home when she made herself into a willing sounding board for her man.

Taking an interest in your husband's work is just one more way of making yourself indispensable to him. When Norman preaches on Sunday mornings, I listen as critically and intelligently as I can. If there is some emphasis that I think is particularly good I tell him about it. I read all his writings and try to offer constructive suggestions. The truth is, neither of us makes any major move or decision without consulting the other. The result is a closeness and a harmony that have grown steadily deeper through the years.

Ours is a partnership that will last as long as we live—and both of us are confident that it will continue unchanged after the transformation known as death. Without that conviction, the future would be hard to face. But we have it, strong and unshakable.

Dear Jennie,

The chapter you just read about being a business consultant to your husband was short, but important. Admittedly, it was written primarily for married women who don't work. I know that you work full time at a career of your own, as do millions of women across the land. It would be unreasonable to expect you to become very involved in your husband's business affairs. And yet...

And yet why can't there be a mutual interest on the part of married couples who work? Why can't each partner learn enough about the other's career or profession to be knowledgeable and helpful and a good sounding board? I don't think that's impossible at all. In fact, I think it's essential. If a marriage is to be a really close one, there can't be a total division when it comes to careers. Inevitably, to some extent, you are married to your husband's job, just as he is married to yours.

This brings me to a subject I didn't touch on in the book, although I should have. It's the problem of jealousy in marriage. I don't mean sexual jealousy. I mean the jealousy that can begin to raise its ugly head when a woman's career in the business or professional world begins to outshine that of her husband.

Ideally a man should give encouragement and support to his wife even if her career tends to overshadow his own. But this is hard for some men to do. The traditional concept of the male as the chief provider in the family is still very much alive in many masculine hearts. If the woman makes more money or seems to be achieving more importance in the outside world, such a man may feel threatened or diminished. And it's very hard to stay in love when that situation is allowed to arise.

Perhaps it hasn't arisen in your case, Jennie, but if there is friction, discord, or trouble of any kind in a marriage it's wise to look at this area and make sure it's not where the trouble is coming from. Common sense tells us that a man should feel proud of a wife who achieves as much in her career as he does in his, or even more. But sometimes he doesn't, because of hidden insecurities within himself. Then it becomes the wife's task to understand his reactions and help him overcome them if she possibly can.

So the fourteenth secret for staying in love is this: **Guard against jealousy over careers.** This can be accomplished by staying interested in each other's jobs and being good consultants for one another.

Difficult, maybe. But sometimes a necessary part of the difficult art of staying in love.

With affection,

Ruth

15

The Most Difficult Problem In Marriage

PEOPLE sometimes ask me, "What is the most difficult problem in human relations that you and your husband are called upon to solve?" I'm not sure that I can give a final answer, but certainly one of the most common is the marriage that's in jeopardy because one of the partners is being or has been unfaithful to the other.

Let me make this clear right at the start: I have no sympathy for adulterers. I have no patience with the sophisticates who condone or excuse infidelity on the grounds of "situation ethics" or any other consideration. To me, the married partner who is unfaithful is breaking the laws of God and man. It is never justified. It is always sinful, always immoral, always wrong.

I know that a great deal of infidelity exists in our society. But I also think that to some extent it has been overplayed. I know there are men who chase women in order to bolster a shaky ego or to reassure themselves about a doubtful masculinity. And there are women who drift from one affair to another in an effort to fill some deep psychological void within themselves. But I think that men are mostly monogamous—and women are too. I believe the typical hard-working, decent American (or Briton, or Spaniard, or Filipino, for that matter) would rather limit himself to one sex partner, a wife whom he loves, than not. Infidelity is not natural for him. It's unnatural. It's immoral.

It's unnatural and immoral for his wife, too. Something deep inside the average woman fears infidelity and flinches from it. What she feels is not fear of the possible consequences so much as the fear of self-condemnation, self-disgust. That is to say, her soul—her spiritual self—reacts against immorality. Love, wifehood, goodness, are built into her by the Creator. I once heard of an unfaithful wife who came home late one afternoon after spending a couple of hours in some hotel room with her lover. She looked through the window of her own living room and saw her husband sitting on the floor by the fire, playing checkers with their little boy, waiting for her to come home. The pang of guilt, shame, and misery that this woman felt was so acute that in that instant, she abandoned her lover and her love affair and never went back to them. It always seemed to me that that was a true portrayal of the basic feminine reaction to adultery.

As for the average husband, he knows perfectly well that extramarital sex is usually an unsatisfactory and furtive business where the momentary thrill is not worth the risk, the trouble, the emotional (and sometimes the financial) investment. Presumably he has worked hard for a number of years to build a home, raise a family, establish a place for himself in a society which, however permissive it has become, still has certain standards and certain rules. Why jeopardize all that for a little short-term excitement? The price tag is too high, unless—and this is the key point—unless something is seriously wrong with his married life, unless there is some unfilled emotional vacuum, unless there is some deep anger or resentment that is demanding this form of retaliation.

In other words, when a husband or a wife jumps out of the corral, one way or another they have been goaded or prodded into making the leap.

I believe that there are thousands of homes—maybe millions—where the seeds of infidelity exist in the form of irritations, maladjustments, small areas of disagreement that can grow into a tangle of weeds that can choke any marriage. I'm convinced that when infidelity has become an imminent threat or an actuality in a marriage, it's because nobody recognized these warning signs. Nobody dealt with these early symptoms. Nobody took an emotional inventory that might have made changes and remedies possible while there was still time.

People think that it's the big, drastic things that destroy marriage, and I'll admit it usually looks that way. But it's really the little things that cause the big things. A woman may divorce her husband because she learns that he's sleeping with his secretary, or is keeping a whole harem of mistresses. But if she could trace the causality back far enough, she might discover that it all began because she couldn't be bothered to put the cap back on the toothpaste—even though she knew that capless toothpaste tubes drove her husband crazy. Of course, it's not that simple, but little adjustments often prevent major problems.

Just the other day a woman from out of town whom I know slightly came up to me and started complaining bitterly because her husband had stopped escorting her to church. They had been married for twenty years, she said, and her husband had always gone to church with her. Now, suddenly, he refused to go any more. She said she thought he had lost his mind, and it was obvious that she wanted me to think so too and agree with her so that she could relay this confirmation without delay to her mindless mate.

"Does he tell you why he won't go?" I asked.

"No," she snapped. "He has no reason. He just won't go."

"Well," I said, "he must have some reason. Perhaps the minister did or said something that offended him." (This is the first thing a minister's wife thinks of!)

"No," she said. "He has no reason. He's just doing it to annoy me! He knows I don't like to sit by myself in church. So that's why he won't go."

That's why *you're* annoyed, I thought, because things aren't the way *you* want them. Aloud I said mildly, "Have you told him this?"

"Of course," she said. "I tell him all the time!"

"Since you've asked for my advice," I said, "I'll give it to you. Stop nagging your husband about this. Go to church alone, or with a friend. Pray to understand your husband better and to be able to communicate with him better. Try putting into practice the religious principles you learn at church. In other words, be patient, tolerant, and kind. Stop thinking about yourself. Try thinking about your husband. If you do, I'm sure you'll be back together—in church and everywhere else. If you don't, I think you'll find yourself without an escort more and more often."

Time and time again Norman and I have seen a marriage go on the rocks because one partner was determined to change the other—and the other could not change. I remember one couple in particular where the wife was the dissatisfied one. She was a rather ambitious person who wanted a heaping measure of the so-called good things of life: money, clothes, cars, travel, social position, and so on. Her husband, who sold real estate, was an easygoing person. He saw no reason to work twelve hours a day when he could get by with six. He was happier puttering around in his basement workshop than having dinner at the country club. He had two or three close friends, and that was good enough for him. He didn't care whether his activities were reported on the society page of the newspaper or not.

For years this wife kept hounding her husband to work harder, make more money, amount to something. When he refused to do all these things, she began to complain more and more to anyone who would listen to her. Quite often this included Norman and me, because she knew her husband admired Norman, and she thought that if Norman backed up her criticism it might have some effect.

One day, I remember, she was listing her husband's deficiencies to Norman with even more vehemence than usual. Not only was Fred lazy, she said, but he was sloppy. He was untidy. He spilled pipe tobacco and ashes on everything. And not only that, he drank too much. He was turning into a real alcoholic.

At this, my usually patient husband spoke up rather loudly. "Marilyn," he said, "I know Fred pretty well. He may not be a man who's going to set the world on fire, and he may spill ashes occasionally, but he is not a boor and he's not an alcoholic. He is a good husband and a good provider. At least, he has been so far. But I don't think he will be much longer, because you are going to drive him away. He wants a quiet, peaceful home. No man can stand the kind of criticism and disapproval that you're handing out. You're going to break up your marriage by insisting on change just because you want things the way you want them."

"He'd never break up our marriage," said Marilyn angrily.

"You're the one," Norman told her, "who's breaking up the marriage. What's more, you're the one who is going to suffer most when it is broken. Fred will go right on having his work and his hobbies and his friends. But what will you have? Not much! I can see you right now, old and lonely and bitter. And you'll still be blaming Fred—for not being something he never was!"

What happened to that marriage? Exactly what Norman predicted. It did break up. We still see them, separately, from time to time. Fred is by himself, but he actually seems a happier person. Marilyn, who never remarried, is lonely and bitter. And it was all so unnecessary! What Marilyn needed was not a go-getter husband, or more money, or more glamor in her life. What she needed was the determination to make her marriage work, using the raw materials that were available. But she never did this. So the marriage died.

The sad and ironic thing is that I'm sure Marilyn could have brought about some of the changes she so ardently desired. Not fundamental personality changes in her husband, perhaps, but surely some of the lesser ones. Pipe ashes, for example. If she had told Fred, quietly and lovingly, that this was something that did upset her, something that it was within his power to correct, he might have listened to her. If perhaps in exchange she had offered to stop doing something in the same category, change some small habit of her own that annoyed him, I'm sure he would have shown the necessary appreciation.

I heard, once, of a marriage counselor in Honolulu who always urges a quarreling couple to write down their pet peeves about each other. He studies each list. Then he draws up a contract for the couple to sign, a contract that will last for a week. If the wife will agree to cut down her cigarettes to ten per day, the husband will help her with the dishes three nights a week. If he will talk to her at breakfast instead of reading the paper, she will stop wearing curlers in her hair. That sort of thing. At the end of the week he calls them in. If they have honored the contract, it remains in force and some new, carefully balanced conditions are added. Apparently this give-and-take technique has been effective in saving a lot of marriages.

I realize that the points I've been trying to make in this chapter are simple and that they've been made before. But I think they're worth repeating to anyone—especially any woman—who wants a marriage to work.

Watch for the small areas of friction and try to eliminate them before they can generate major centrifugal forces.

Don't expect perfection from the person you married, because you can't offer it yourself.

Try to control you own ego, at least to the point of seeing both sides of any controversy or disagreement.

Study your man and try to supply his basic emotional needs.

If you can do these things, the specter of infidelity need never cast a shadow across the adventure of being a wife.

Dear Jennie,

Sometimes I think the reason adultery is regarded with such repugnance in virtually every society is not just that it is a violation of the laws of God and man, but also because it represents the ultimate in dishonesty and deceit. You never find a case of adultery that does not involve some kind of furtive deception. No wife is going to be so brazen as to flaunt her infidelity publicly. No husband – no normal man, anyway – is going to say to his wife, "Yes, I'm having an affair – so what?" There is always a conspiracy to hide the truth with evasions or lies or some other form of dishonesty.

With this in mind, I would suggest that one strong defense against infidelity in marriage is total honesty. If husband and wife can get into the habit of never lying to each other, even in the smallest things, then they are very unlikely to deceive in larger things.

There are other defenses against infidelity that one reads or hears about from time to time. Let's say a woman senses (as you do, Jennie) that the romance is draining out of her marriage. So she tries to make herself more appealing, with a new hair-do, new clothes, new perfume, and so on.

There's nothing wrong, certainly, with making yourself as attractive as you can. Every wife should do it. But no matter how attractive and seductive such a wife becomes, chances are there will always be women somewhere who are more so. If physical attraction alone is the bait that lures a man away, the wife may well be fighting a losing battle.

Furthermore, these well-meant efforts may keep her from looking for more basic causes of the trouble. Is she being too selfish or too self-centered in the daily give-and-take of marriage? (These questions apply to husbands just as much as to wives!) Does she outshine or overshadow him with no concern or regard for his feelings?

Has she given him cause for legitimate grievances that are slowly turning his love into resentment? All these things are likely to be of more importance than mere sex appeal or lack of it.

The subject is enormous, Jennie. No one could begin to do justice to it in one short letter. But if I had to give one piece of advice it would center around this question of honesty. Thus, I would say the fifteenth secret of staying in love is: **Be totally honest.**

In your relationship with Jack, never lie, never dissemble, never deceive. And expect the same from him. This will strengthen your marriage more than you can imagine.

Total honesty leads to total trust. And that's one of the sure-fire secrets of staying in love.

Your friend,

Ruth

16

One Afternoon In Winter

I'M finishing this book in the same place where I started it, our old white farmhouse on Quaker Hill in Pawling, New York. Inside the house, all is the same except that now a fire is crackling on the hearth. Outside all is different. The soft greens of April have been replaced by the stark blacks, whites, and grays of winter. Snow lies deep along our fence-rows, and the great maples lift their gaunt arms against the sky. At night the stars blaze above fields so quiet that you can hear the silence sing. December is a good time to finish things.

It seems like a long time since that dark-haired girl in the psychology class stood up to challenge my views on marriage. But I'm glad now that she did. I'm glad, too, that Norman encouraged and supported me in the writing of this book which is my answer to her and people like her. Without his help I could never have finished it.

I've found that by the time you're through with it, a book becomes something like an old friend, rewarding at times, demanding at others, cantankerous and difficult on bad days, fun and exciting on good ones. We have talked about this book and worked on it here at the farm, on innumerable two-hour drives into New York City, on short trips and on long transoceanic plane flights. We have made rough drafts in London and revised them in Madrid and Rome. We have written sections in Holland, Michigan, and discarded them in Amsterdam, Holland. The final result, as I predicted to Norman, is rather like a patchwork quilt, but I hope the central idea and message have come through.

As I've indicated many times, my whole intent and purpose have been simply to affirm my faith in the ancient and honorable estate known as marriage, to try to answer some of the critics, to persuade some of the doubters and skeptics that, far from being a burden or a bore, it can be a great adventure. Like all true adventures, it has its risks and its hazards, but without these it *would* be a bore.

I have tried to convey, furthermore, my conviction that the success or failure of any marriage depends primarily on the wife. She is—or should be—the one who largely determines the emotional climate in which a marriage grows and flourishes. Regardless of what the feminists may say or think, in our society the chief responsibility of most women is the creation and maintenance of a home. And the whole fabric of our culture is determined by how well or how badly they do the job.

In saying this, I certainly am not downgrading women. Instead, I am assigning to them the key role in civilization as we know it. Men may supply the energies that keep the ship of state moving forward. But women are the rudder—and the rudder determines where the ship will go.

I also hope I have managed to get across the importance of constant effort, study, compromise, and adjustment if a marriage is to grow into the kind of relationship that I know it can be. In a way, marriage is like religion—it works when you work at it. A good marriage doesn't just happen. It has to be made to happen. But when you really work at it, and it really works, nothing in the world pays such dividends or brings such rewards.

Now that I'm at the end of the book, I keep thinking of little episodes that I wish I had included—just the small, warm, wonderful moments of family living that are the dividends I'm talking about. Like the time, for instance, when our John was a little boy of seven or eight and had an accident in which his ear was cut very badly. We rushed him to the hospital where they put him on the operating table. In preparation, they emptied his pockets of all his boyish treasures—marbles and old candies and a pocket-knife and bits of string. I can see them to this day and still feel the tug at my heart.

He lay there, so pale and uncomplaining, while we held his hands, all smudged and dirty from playing. Norman, thinking of all the times he had sent John away from the dinner table with orders to wash his hands, said suddenly—because the emotion he was feeling had to go somewhere—"John, I'll *never* make you go and wash your hands at mealtime again!"

Well, of course, the ear was patched up with no permanent damage, and the day finally came when John appeared at the dinner table unwashed. "John," said his father absently, "go and wash your hands." Whereupon John fixed him with a reproachful gaze. "You *promised!*" he said. I forget now what compromise we made, and perhaps the story has little significance for others, but it has a lot for me.

There is also the time when I was in our New York apartment and Norman was filling a speaking engagement on the West Coast. At four in the morning my bedside telephone rang. Dazed with sleep, I picked it up and heard

Norman's voice coming all the way from Seattle. "Ruth," he said, and I could tell he was upset, "are you all right?"

"All right?" I repeated numbly. "Why, yes. I'm fine."

"Are you *sure* you're fine?" insisted Norman. "Do you *really* feel all right?"

"Of course," I answered, now sitting bolt upright and wide-awake. "I feel great. What's the matter with you?"

It seemed that Norman had come back to the hotel after making his speech, had gone to sleep, and had had a nightmare in which I was terribly ill—in fact, dying. It had frightened him so that he had seized the phone and called me to make sure that it was only a dream.

We talked for a while, and I forget what else we said, but I'll never forget my husband's last words. "Ruth," he said, "you have the sweetest voice in the world..."

Once a man and a woman have attained this kind of closeness, it will last as long as they live.

Dear Jennie,

Well, we have come to the end of the book, and so this will be my last letter to you for a while. It will not be the end of our friendship, surely, because I think we will always keep in touch. But I feel I have kept the promise I made to you. I'm afraid I haven't always had time to do justice to these little letters, but I hope you've found them helpful.

I think perhaps you have indeed benefited, Jennie, because the letters you have written in reply have changed in tone as the weeks have gone by. I've sensed in them a trend away from pessimism to a growing note of optimism and hope.

I wish you'd write me one last letter, telling me how things are now with your marriage. I want to know not only how things are now, but how the future looks to you. I'm asking this because I believe the vision you have of your marriage as it will be one, two, or five years from now has a lot to do with the way the marriage is going to be. If you see yourself moving steadily into a better relationship with Jack, more loving and more understanding, then that goal will tend to actualize itself. On the other hand, if you resign yourself to increasing tension, a gradual disintegration of your marriage, or perhaps even eventual divorce, then these bleak expectations are likely to become realities.

Philosophers have always told us that we are what we think. Actually we don't need philosophers to tell us that, because deep in our hearts most of us know this already. This brings me to my last point. The last secret of staying in love, Jennie, is this: **Anticipate happiness and not disappointment.** Your attitude is the key. Visualize the path of marriage leading upward, not downward. Forget any unhappiness that lurks in the past. Focus on the future—yours and Jack's. This will certainly help your marriage to be what you want it to be.

You know, Jennie, it seems like a long time since our plane touched down in Los Angeles that day so many weeks ago. To be sure, a great deal has happened to both of us during that time. I hope the encouraging things that have been happening in your marriage will continue to increase.

I remember from our conversation as we talked that day, that you told me you need things spelled out plainly. Although all of the secrets are in the letters I wrote you, I thought you might want to have a final list of the things we discovered by reading the book. So here is the list you asked for – here are the "secrets of staying in love."

1. Be committed.
2. Accept your mate.
3. Think of your mate before you think of yourself.
4. Create special times for undisturbed romance.
5. Keep God at the center of your marriage.
6. Be a good climate-arranger.
7. Pray.
8. Study your in-laws.
9. Honestly appraise your own personality.
10. Appreciate your mate.
11. Blend your lives together.
12. Learn to be an effective shock absorber.
13. Learn to laugh together.
14. Guard against jealousy over careers.
15. Be totally honest.
16. Anticipate happiness and not disappointment.

I hope these secrets will continue to help you. Use them, Jennie. You can have that special, warm, loving marriage that you long to have. Strive for it. Believe in it. Reach for it. Fight for it. Pray for it. Persevere until you get it.

God bless you, Jennie. May He keep you and Jack in His loving care – now and always. You will continue to be in my prayers.

Ruth

Dear Mrs. Peale,

First let me thank you once again for all the effort and kindness that you have shown in the letters you have written to me. I don't know how you found the time or the persistence to keep your promise week after week, but I'm so glad you did. I think it's probably fair to say that those little letters have saved our marriage.

This past weekend Jack and I went on a short trip to Canada. No work, no business appointments, no conflict – just us. It was like a second honeymoon – a new beginning even better than our first honeymoon. We have learned so much – thanks to you – about the secrets of staying in love.

I say "we" because Jack also read all the letters you sent. He wasn't aware of our correspondence at first. At that point we weren't really communicating much at all. But gradually he began to sense a change in me. When he asked what was causing it, I told him about our meeting on the plane. After that he began to read the letters too.

I think the letter that made the biggest impression on Jack was the one that spoke about man and woman being complementary halves of a divinely planned team or unit. I remember his saying, "Yes, that's right. If the two halves really fit like pieces of a jigsaw puzzle, then everything is more than doubled. Love, talent, brain-power, understanding, patience, strength...everything." Then he also said, "The cracks in our jigsaw puzzle have grown too wide, Jennie. Let's try fitting ourselves back together again." That was the turning point I think.

I can't tell you what this new and growing sense of closeness has meant to Jack and me, Mrs. Peale. I think we are beginning to discover the kind of closeness that you and your husband have had all these years. I truly think the hidden hand of God was behind our meeting on that airplane. And I thank Him for it.

We expect to spend the rest of our years staying very

much in love. We know that we still have a long way to go. We can't expect to solve all our problems overnight. But we know that with God's help, we can make our marriage work. We see a future ultimately full of promise and happiness.

Jack and I will always remember you with admiration and affection. Thank you again for your love and concern for us and our marriage. I hope you continue to reach people like us who really only need a little advice and direction to save their marriage.

Gratefully,

Jennie